Tribalism and Prejudice

Tribalism and Prejudice

The Far-Right and Lessons From History

Simon Bell

ABOUT THE AUTHOR

Simon Bell is a former mental health nurse with over 37 years of National Health Service experience in England. The first 15 years of his career were spent working in hospitals, and included–in old asylum care–looking after severely damaged, elderly survivors of the war in Europe and the Holocaust. These shadows of humanity had eyes that appeared not to see, but had tormented minds that sadly knew and saw too much. That instilled a long-held interest not just in the Holocaust but in the consequences of all hatred and discrimination. For nearly 22 years he worked with mentally-disordered offenders, and has dealt with most types of criminal behaviour, witnessed the consequences of crime, and dealt with those who have experienced the extremes of personal trauma. Aside from a clinical role, he also helped to deliver training to a range of mental health and other disciplines in helping them to understand and deal with patients who have experienced childhood and adult sexual abuse. In the summer of 2016 Simon retired from health care. He is now studying for an MA in Second World War Studies: Conflict-Societies-Holocaust.

Simon prides himself on not having any formal allegiance to religious or political parties or groups. He is however, dedicated to challenging intolerance and hatred in all of its forms, and seeking to ensure that those who might be targeted or oppressed are supported and cared for. He has been fortunate to have visited Auschwitz-Birkenau on a number of occasions, as well as other sites in Poland that are associated with the Holocaust He has spent time meeting and exchanging correspondence with survivors and scholars, historians and others who share his interest. He does not pray, but he wishes and hopes for a better, more tolerant, and more caring world.

This book is dedicated to my younger brother Andy. My best friend through my early years, and someone I admired and loved greatly until his untimely demise. Andy was larger than life: a polyglot and a polymath in equal measure; big in stature, strong as an ox, and with an enormous heart. His knowledge, wisdom, zest for life, and passion for his family will be unequalled by anyone I know. This is for you Bro.

Andy Bell–March 1963 to August 2017

Acknowledgements

I am grateful to friends, associates, colleagues, scholars and historians who have supported me through hours of research and helped nurture the need to put thoughts on paper.

I am fortunate to have met and got to know survivors of the Holocaust, one of the darkest periods in human history. I offer personal and heartfelt thanks to Kitty Hart-Moxon–a most inspirational woman, whom I feel humbled and honoured to know and to share a friendship with.

I would like to thank my wife Bev and my sons Josh and Ben above all. Not many wives accept a husband travelling hundreds of miles just to talk to someone or tolerate him researching endlessly from a houseful of Holocaust and genocide related material. Without their support this book would never have happened.

Contents

INTRODUCTION

This book–in reality an essay–is written out of concern that societies across the westernised democracies appear at times to have failed in their duty to remember and to learn from the lessons of the past. In living memory the world, including continental Europe, has been torn apart by brutal wars, and has witnessed terrible genocides. Yet Europe, which has largely been at peace for over seventy years, is awash with far-right nationalism and hostility towards others.

The United States, always a beacon to the rest of the world, has become seen as being increasingly isolationist and a country where populism which would have previously been condemned, has become normal and acceptable. America, the land of President Kennedy, and Dr Martin Luther King Jr; where the civil rights movement caught the attention of the world; the land of liberators, and home of the United Nations, is a place that, in 2017, the Ku Klux Klan, neo-Nazis, and white supremacists, some brandishing swastikas, feel emboldened to march once more. When Holocaust survivors express dismay, people should listen.

The United Nations acknowledges the genocides that encompassed the Holocaust-during which concerted efforts were made to eradicate the Jews from Europe-and also Cambodia, Rwanda, Darfur, and at Srebrenica in Bosnia. In time other conflicts will be seen as genocidal. Many factors contribute to genocide, but foremost is the total contempt for fellow human beings and a view that not only are they undeserving of the rights, protections, and dignities others hold dear; they are also deemed to be unworthy of life. Time and again, after each genocide, the world says 'never again', and yet repeatedly the same horrors occur.

It is often said that those who fail to learn the lessons of past mistakes are destined to repeat them. Genocide and hate crime do not belong solely to one side of the political spectrum. Communist regimes up until the end of the Cold War were notoriously brutal and responsible for millions of innocent lives being lost. North Korea is still a land with an oppressed and fearful population at constant risk of being embroiled in a self-destructive war. Some left wing politicians and groups buy into and promote some of the same hatreds and intolerances that the far-right are condemned for.

However, common factors in genocide have been extreme tribalism, prejudice, nationalism, and populist ideals that allow the ready targeting of others living within a given society. Populist nationalism alone will not lead to genocide. Civil unrest, recession, mass-unemployment, war, a breakdown of the rule of law, and a sense of external threat or internal danger, all contribute. Tribalism and prejudice can be seen as normal, and possibly, within limits, they may even be healthy and a protection against real, as opposed to perceived, danger. But when tribalism and prejudice lead to hatred, intolerance and contempt, the consequences are invariably harmful, and can be devastating. This book will explore aspects of this, with particular attention being focused on the National Socialism of Hitler's Germany, the war in former Yugoslavia, the rise of the far-right and populist nationalism, and some discussion about the psychology and sociology associated with prejudice and hate.

The author has visited Auschwitz-Birkenau on a number of occasions, as well as other sites in Poland associated with the Holocaust. He has spent many hours in the company of Holocaust survivors and has heard first-hand their detailed accounts of life leading up to, during, and following the Holocaust. He has met, in his former professional role, survivors of other genocides and conflicts. He has studied genocide, particularly the Holocaust, for many years and has often considered, but not been able to articulate, what leads apparently normal societies to become bestial places of slaughter. In endeavouring to understand this a period of research was undertaken. Understanding hate and tribalism does not excuse the harm it causes, but it may help to explain why some societies degenerate into places in which minorities can be dehumanised and slaughtered. As a mental health nurse the author spent 22 years dealing with suspects, defendants and offenders from the time of arrest through to the conclusion of criminal proceedings. He encountered many types of crime–from low level disorder through to serious violence, sexual harm, and murder-and a wide range of harm caused and experienced. With many offenders the route into criminality, and the socially abnormal and unacceptable nature of their behaviour, could often be explained. But explaining the apparent normality of mass hatred and intolerance is less obvious. This book seeks to find some answers and to ask some questions about the perceived acceptability of hate today. It is hoped that the research referred to herein, and the opinions and observations offered, will equip readers to undertake their own research and that they will be able to challenge intolerance through constructive, reasoned, and thoughtful arguments.

PREAMBLE

This book will examine and consider whether hatred, tribalism and populist nationalism are normal. Are they dangerous, or are they anomalies from the parameters that permit the safe, communal cooperation of society? Humans by nature seem to function and thrive more successfully when they engage together for the greater good of all. Yet, in living memory–and in older history–there have been wars, conflicts, hostilities, and genocides borne out of fierce, tribal loyalty to one group and violent animosity towards another. This has been most grotesquely demonstrated in genocides and the legislative acts, or societal deeds, of demonising, ostracising, and isolating any element of the community deemed to be less worthy than the majority or the more powerful group. Consideration will be specifically given to the National Socialism of Hitler's Germany, the genocide in Bosnia, the rise of the far-right in westernised democracies, and the prevalence of populist nationalism in those societies. The discussion will also encompass the concepts of absolutism, literalism, and fundamentalism that may have a significant bearing on the actions of those who deem others to be lesser human beings, to be undeserving of the liberties and rights afforded to the majority or dominant group, and ultimately to be unworthy of life.

Further discussion will look at the shift from the anti-Semitism of National Socialism in the years until the conclusion of the Second World War, the change of hate targets, the legitimising of hate and hate groups, and the potential for harm, and ultimately genocide, that this may or may not indicate.

There are no easy answers. Genocide and the hate that leads to it originate from varied and complex factors, some of which can be seen to be common and replicated, some of which are unique to any given society. The shared factors do allow some potential for legislative control, and for societies and communities to identify and address causative issues and to prevent harm before it occurs. Sadly, history shows that often intervention occurs after the events of mass harm–Bosnia and Rwanda are prime modern examples–and that warnings, when they are given, can go unheeded. There is surely an indisputable truth that to prevent history being repeated, lessons must be learned from past events, and that the best guide to potential behaviour is previous behaviour.

In western democratic societies today there has been a rise in populist nationalism that has sought to apportion blame for the ills of nation states on the actions of others from outside of the nation; be they foreign powers, migrants and refugees, or from within the nation; racial and religious minorities, political groups, and others. Elements of the popular press in the UK use the language of implied treason by describing those who opposed Brexit (as an example) and even judges upholding the law as enemies. Most notably the Daily Mail on 3 November 2016 had a headline which included: *Enemies of the people: Fury over 'out of touch' judges who have 'declared war on democracy.*[1] Less than

---

1　James Slack, Political Editor, *Daily Mail*, 3 November 2016, http://www.dailymail.co.uk/news/article-3903436/Enemies

a month earlier the Sunday Express headline of 11 October 2016 stated: *'Europhile' Treasury accused of 'acting as a fifth column' in Government over Brexit warning.*[2] In the past enemies of the state or perceived fifth columnists were incarcerated, deprived of civil liberties, and even executed for the crime of disagreement and offering an alternative political view. This discussion does not start from a premise that such radical and destructive measures are a risk today, but deprivation of liberties, and harmful government actions tend to develop gradually rather than immediately. The press can be a factor in the success or failure of any government policy or stance. In a democratic society the press needs to be free of government control and influence. Journalists across the political spectrum should be able to freely, honestly, and openly question the executives of high office, hold politicians to account, and offer an alternative opinion and interpretation of the official policies of government. In totalitarian states the press does not have such freedom. In recent months press autonomy has been dismissed in some quarters as fake news. Merely stating that news is false or biased because it is contrary to the view of politicians and their supporters does not evidentially and provably make it fake. There is a risk, unless such a mind-set is robustly challenged, that government propaganda dictates the flow of news, rather than the flow of news being instrumental in reflecting, scrutinising, and criticising governments.

-people-Fury-touch-iudges-defied-17-4m-Brexit-voters-trigger -constitutional crisis.html, accessed 23 July 2017

2   Greg Heffer, Political Reporter, *Sunday Express,* 11 October 2016, http://www.express.co.uk/news/politics/719871/Brexit-Treasury-Brexit-warning-EU-single-market-66billion-Patrick-Minford-fifth-column, accessed 23 July 2017

It is imperative that the press and political opponents are allowed to disagree with governments, with decisions made, and with policies, without it being implied that they are somehow guilty of treason or enemies of the state.

'Make America Great Again', 'Take Back Control' and other mantras of a similar style have been the clarion call of modern nationalism in the United States, the United Kingdom, Europe, and elsewhere. They imply that control and power has been ceded to some vague 'other' without the specifics ever needing to be clarified. Whilst the independence of states is necessary, the reality is that global trade and international cooperation depends upon mutually beneficial agreements and standards of interaction. Isolationism may appeal to populist nationalism but it does not reflect the realities of the world today.

It is important to discover whether individuals and societies are more prone than others towards intolerance and violence and whether a racist personality or tribal intolerance is the norm. There may be similarities in the attitudes that prevailed during the Nazi regime and in the civil war in Former Yugoslavia. There appears to be a rise in the acceptability of far-right and populist nationalism. Populist attitudes of intolerance towards refugees and religious or racial minorities today, may be comparable to previous more harmful periods in modern history. Whether there are lessons that can obviously be learned, warnings that can be heeded, or actions that can be taken to maintain some of the fundamental and expected freedoms of democratic societies is an area to explore and discuss.

When the Second World War concluded the allied victors sought to impose punishments on the Axis powers. This was most notably demonstrated at the International Military Tribunal and subsequent trials at Nuremberg. The

United Nations also ratified Conventions on the Crime of Genocide and the Universal Declaration of Human Rights. The main discussion of this book will commence by considering these pieces of legislation and the broader definition of genocide.

The Genocide Convention

The United Nations Convention on the Prevention and Punishment of the Crime of Genocide was signed by the General Assembly in Paris on 9 December 1948, following a unanimous vote. It strayed somewhat from the original concepts of Raphael Lemkin who had first proposed that such a crime existed and should be punished.[3] The Convention's final text made clear that genocide, whether it occurred in peacetime or war, in domestic circumstances or abroad, was a punishable and extraditable offence under international law.[4] It further clarified that anyone, whether they be a private person or public official, who committed genocide, or was complicit through incitement or conspiracy, would be made subject to prosecution.[5] Article II of the Convention defined genocide as:

> Genocide means any of the following acts committed with intent to destroy, in whole or in part, a national, ethnical, racial, or religious group, as such:

---

3 David Mayers, Humanity in 1948: The Genocide Convention and the Universal Declaration of Human Rights, *Diplomacy and Statecraft*, 26, (2015), p. 452

4 *Ibid*, p. 452

5 ibid, p. 452

a. Killing members of the group;
b. Causing serious bodily or mental harm to members of the group;
c. Deliberately inflicting on the group conditions of life calculated to bring about its physical destruction in whole or in part;
d. Imposing measures intended to prevent births within the group;
e. Forcibly transferring children of the group to another group.[6]

Hilary Earl notes that prior to the Convention there was a complex relationship between the idea of genocide as articulated by Lemkin, particularly between 1945 and 1949 during the thirteen Nuremberg Trials. This included how those working on the trials perceived Lemkin's ideas and the crime he was trying to get adopted as law.[7] As Earl observes, although no one was indicted at Nuremberg for genocide, the prosecutors understood that the concept of genocide meant race murder and extermination, with the targeted murder of Europe's Jews and other populations.[8] Despite having the opportunity to establish an international legal precedent, the prosecutors did not fully employ the term genocide, and instead used criminal law to prosecute the Nazi defendants.[9] For the Nuremberg prosecutors

---

6 ibid, p. 452
7 Hilary Earl, Prosecuting Genocide before the Genocide Convention: Raphael Lemkin and the Nuremberg Trials, 1945–1949, Journal of Genocide Research, 2013 Vol. 15, No. 3 (2013), p. 319
8 Ibid, p. 319
9 Ibid, p. 319

it was easier to seek proof that the defendants had committed murder in the context of the racist ideology of the Third Reich regime, rather than seeking to prove a newly defined and complex crime involving the murder and persecution of one group by another group. There was a concern that prosecuting using a law that was not yet codified risked causing problems with the entire Nuremberg project, and as such, whilst Lemkin's ideas about genocide impacted the thinking of prosecutors, they were not turned not turned into positive law at the International Military Tribunal (IMT).[10]

Although Lemkin had recognised that genocide could be a singular violent event, he also conceived and wrote about it as a process. Lemkin believed that what distinguished genocide from other forms of forced assimilation and national oppression was the physical destruction of the targeted group. He was aware that there were many ways to destroy a group besides physically killing members of that group such as destroying national forms of self-government, killing the intelligentsia, imposing the oppressor's language and education (forced assimilation), depriving targeted groups of the ability to be self-sustaining, and imposing biological policies so that the targeted group will be unable to procreate.[11]

In 1996 Gregory H. Stanton of Genocide Watch presented a briefing paper to the US State Department. Originally it was referred to as The Eight Stages of Genocide, but since then Discrimination and Persecution have been added to make it The Ten Stages of Genocide.[12] Stanton suggested

---

10 Ibid, p. 319

11 ibid, p. 321

12 Gregory H. Stanton, Genocide Watch, The Ten Stages of Genocide, (2013), http://www.genocidewatch.org/10stagesofgenocide.ppt, accessed 27 July 2017

that Genocide is a process that develops in ten stages that are predictable but not inexorable. In his view preventative measures can stop the process at each stage. He further suggested that the process is not linear, that stages may occur simultaneously, but that logically later stages would be preceded by earlier stages and that all stages continue to operate throughout the process.[13] Stanton and Genocide Watch's ten stages are Classification, Symbolization, Discrimination, Dehumanization, Organization, Polarization, Preparation, Persecution, Extermination and Denial.[14] The Stages are worthy of consideration individually as they will become relevant when comparing the attitudes and actions in various known genocides with some of the attitudes that will be discussed as being apparent in modern contemporary political thinking, tribalism, hate, and intolerance.

1. CLASSIFICATION: This recognises that all cultures have categories to distinguish groups into us and them by virtue of ethnicity, race, religion or nationality, such as German and Jew or Hutu and Tutsi. Bipolar societies that do not have mixed societies, such as Rwanda and Burundi, are most likely to have genocide. The most effective preventative measure at this stage is to develop institutions that transcend ethnic or racial divisions, that actively promote tolerance and understanding, and that promote classifications that cross divisions. Stanton observes that the Catholic Church could have played such a role in Rwanda, and he suggests that the search for common ground is vital to the early prevention of genocide.[15]

---

13 *ibid*

14 *ibid*

15 *ibid*

2. SYMBOLIZATION: Stanton observes that societies give symbols quite normally to classifications in how groups are referred to or by clothing and style of dress. Such classification and symbolisation does not result in genocide. However, when combined with hatred, symbols may be forced upon unwilling members of pariah groups such as happened with yellow stars for Jews under Nazi rule, or the blue scarf for people from the eastern zone in Cambodia under the rule of the Khmer Rouge. Stanton suggests that to combat symbolisation, hate symbols (such as the swastika) or hate speech can be legally forbidden. Group marking or tribal scarring can also be outlawed. In Bulgaria the symbolism of the yellow star was not enforced which deprived that symbol of its power and significance.[16]

3. DISCRIMINATION: Stanton observes how a dominant group uses law, custom, and political power to deny the rights of other groups. Powerless groups may be denied full civil rights, and educational and employment opportunities as seen with the Nuremberg Laws of 1935 in Nazi Germany. In Myanmar the Rohingya Muslim minority have been denied citizenship rights. Stanton suggests that discrimination on the basis of nationality, ethnicity, race, or religion should be outlawed, and that individuals should be able to take legal action against the state, corporations, and others if their rights are violated.[17]

4. DEHUMANISATION: Stanton describes how this occurs when one group denies the humanity of another group. Members of the victim group are equated with animals,

---

16 *ibid*

17 *ibid*

vermin, insects or diseases. Stanton suggests that dehumanisation helps to overcome normal human revulsion against murder. At this stage hate propaganda is used to vilify the victim group. He further observes that the right to free and protected speech should not be confused with the dehumanisation that incites genocide. Stanton suggests that genocidal societies lack constitutional protection for countervailing speech and should not be treated the same as democracies. He observes that local and international leaders should condemn hate speech and make it culturally unacceptable. He further opines that leaders who incite genocide should be banned from international travel and have foreign finances frozen. Hate radio stations should be shut down, hate propaganda should be banned, and hate crimes and atrocities should be promptly punished.[18]

5. ORGANISATION: Stanton suggests that genocide is always organised, and that this is usually by the state, often with the use of militias to distance the state from responsibility (such as the Janjaweed in Darfur). The organisation can be informal or decentralised as in the case of terrorist groups. He suggests that special army units or militias are often trained and armed. Plans are made for genocidal killings. Stanton offers the opinion that to combat this stage, membership of such militias should be outlawed and their leaders should be denied visas for foreign travel. Stanton suggests that the United Nations should impose arms embargoes on governments and citizens of countries involved in genocidal massacres and create commissions to investigate violations.[19]

---

18 *ibid*
19 *ibid*

6. POLARISATION: Stanton observes that extremists drive groups apart. He gives examples of hate groups broadcasting polarising propaganda, and laws that forbid intermarriage or social interaction. Extremist terrorism groups target moderates, and intimidate and silence those on the centre of politics. Stanton suggests that moderates from the perpetrators' own group are most able to stop genocide and as such are often the first to be arrested and killed. Stanton observes that prevention may require security protection form moderate leaders or assistance to human rights groups. He opines that coups d'état by extremists should be opposed by international sanctions.[20]

7. PREPARATION: Stanton observes that national or perpetrator group leaders often plan genocide as in the cases of the Nazi's Final Solution or the genocide against the Tutsis in Rwanda. Stanton notes that they will often use euphemisms to cloak their intentions such as referring to their objectives as ethnic cleansing, purification, or counter-terrorism. They build armies, train militias and buy weapons. They indoctrinate the populace with fear of the victim groups and make claims such as 'if we don't kill them, they will kill us.' Stanton suggests that prevention should include prosecution for incitement and conspiracy to commit genocide which are both crimes under Article 3 of the Genocide Convention.[21]

8. PERSECUTION: Stanton observes that victims are identified and separated out because of their ethnic or religious identity. Death lists can be drawn up. In state sponsored

---

20 *ibid*

21 *ibid*

genocide, members of the victim groups may be forced to wear identifying symbols, their property can be taken, and they may be segregated into ghettoes, deported into concentration camps, or confined to famine-struck regions and starved. Stanton suggests that this is when genocidal massacres begin. They are acts of genocide because they intentionally destroy part of the group. Stanton further suggests that at this stage a Genocide Emergency must be declared and international military action should take place, followed by the provision of aid and refugee assistance.[22]

9. EXTERMINATION: Stanton suggests that extermination begins and quickly becomes the crime of genocide. To the killers it is extermination because they do not consider their victims to be fully human. Stanton observes that in state-sponsored killings the armed forces will work with militias. Sometimes the genocide results in revenge killings by groups against each other creating what Stanton refers to as 'a downward whirlpool-like cycle of bilateral genocide.' Stanton suggest that at this stage only rapid and overwhelming armed intervention can stop the genocide. He also suggests that real safe areas or refugee escape corridors should be set up with heavily armed international protection–he adds that an unsafe 'safe' area is worse than none at all.[23]

10. DENIAL: Stanton observes that this is the final stage and always follows a genocide. He offers the opinion that it is among the surest indicators of further genocidal massacres. Perpetrators will dig up mass graves, burn bodies, attempt to cover up evidence, and intimidate witnesses. They deny

---

22 *ibid*
23 *ibid*

committing any crimes and often blame events on victims. They will block investigations of the crimes and will continue to govern until driven from power by force when they will flee into exile, and remain safe until captured or a tribunal is established to try them. At trial the evidence can be heard and the perpetrators punished. Stanton realistically notes that national and international tribunals may not deter genocidal killers but with political will to arrest and prosecute them, some may be brought to justice.[24]

Stanton's observations may appear simplistic, but they have an observable validity when considered with what is known about modern genocides and factors that led to such crimes. His ten stages are also worthy of note when considering the rise of populist nationalism and the far-right which will be a substantial part of further discussion in this book.

---

24 *ibid*

The Universal Declaration of Human Rights

The Universal Declaration of Human Rights was adopted as a United Nations (UN) Resolution in 1948, as part of the ongoing international process of establishing legal safeguards after the Second World War. As Margaret E. McGuinness observes, the diplomatic process that led to the adoption of the Declaration began in New York City in 1946.[25] At that time the UN Commission on Human Rights met for the first time and set out the guidelines from which to draft the text which would be adopted by the UN General Assembly resolution in 1948.[26] McGuinness suggests that the writers of the draft Charter were motivated in part by what they perceived as the nexus between the aggression of the Axis powers and the rejection by those regimes of the universality of rights.[27] It was felt that ending war and stabilising peace lay at the centre of the UN legal framework, whilst maintaining peace and security was seen as the work

---

25 Margaret E. McGuinness, Peace v. Justice; The Universal Declaration of Human Rights and the Modern Origins of the Debate, *Diplomatic History,* 35 (5), (2011), p. 749
26 *ibid,* p. 749
27 *ibid,* p. 750

of the UN Security Council which was the only UN body with the power to bind member states to its resolutions.[28]

The International Military Tribunal and the Nuremberg Trials sought to erase certain privileges of sovereignty by removing particular crimes–notably, war crimes and crimes against humanity–from the exclusive jurisdiction of states.[29] One of the goals was to deter future aggression by enforcing individual liability and the removal of individual immunities to prosecution.[30] But as McGuinness observes, Nuremberg focussed on the crime of Nazi aggression and crimes committed in the furtherance of war, and did not take into account the human rights abuses and atrocities committed by the Nazis as part of the peacetime domestic policies of government. It was therefore the war, rather than the acts of atrocity, that led to the imposition of international jurisdiction.[31] To this extent the Nuremberg trial process differed from the subsequent recognition of wider human rights and the imposition of international legal processes to defend those rights and prosecute abuses. As McGuiness elaborates, the first meeting of the Human Rights Commission in May 1946: 'fully realised the importance of achieving and promoting the recognition and observance of human rights and fundamental freedoms for all, in the hope of drawing from the last world war which demanded the sacrifice of so many lives, the lessons which will aid us to achieve the highest aspirations of mankind.'[32]

---

28 *ibid*, p. 750
29 *ibid*, p. 751
30 *ibid*, p. 751
31 *ibid*, p. 751
32 *ibid*, pp. 752–753

The initial session of the Commission recommended that while work began on crafting an international bill of rights, the general principle should be the acceptance of basic human rights in international treaties and peace treaties, and that similar provisions should be accepted by all States, Members of the UN, and any States seeking admission to the UN.[33] The Commission recommended a role for itself in assisting the Security Council by pointing out where violations of human rights may be seen to constitute a threat to the peace. The UN Charter was seen as being complimentary to the UN's broader role in preventing war and was seen as ensuring the human rights were a necessary part of peace agreements.[34]

---

33 *ibid,* pp.752753
34 *ibid,* pp.752753

THE NAZI REGIME–ANTI-SEMITISM, RACISM, CRIMES

The social, economic and political circumstances that led to the rise of National Socialism in Germany after the First World War cannot be compared to western societies today. The attitudes towards others, particularly Jews, are worthy of comparison to the climate of intolerance that appears to have gained legitimacy in some quarters. Hitler established and set out his views on the purity of the Aryan race as he perceived it and of the risks associated with others harming that purity: 'Human culture and civilisation on this continent are inseparably bound up with the presence of the Aryan. If he dies out or declines, the dark veils of an age without culture will again descend on the globe.'[35]

As David Cesarani observes-and this is worthy of comparison to the situation of some minority populations in Europe and elsewhere today-the self-identifying Jewish population of the German Republic in the early twentieth century numbered roughly 525,000, and of that number approximately 100,000 were recent immigrants from

---

35 Adolf Hitler, Mein Kampf, Translated by Ralph Manheim, (London:2014), p. 348

Eastern Europe, known as the Ostjuden.[36] In contrast, most German born Jews could trace their roots back centuries and were well integrated into German society.[37] Although there were areas of Orthodox Judaism, for most Jews their religious practice was diluted. For example each December the typical German Jewish family not only lit candles for the festival of Chanukkah, they also had a Christmas tree at home.[38] There were high rates of marriage outside of the Jewish faith with 25 per cent of Jewish men and 16 per cent of Jewish women marrying outside of their traditional community. Indeed, the children of these mixed-faith marriages were invariably raised as Christians.[39]

Hitler could not sanction the idea of mixed relationships. He opined that: 'Every animal mates only with a member of the same species.'[40] Elaborating on this theme Hitler stated: 'Any crossing of the beings not at exactly the same level produces a medium between the level of the parents…such mating is contrary to the will of nature for a higher breeding of all life.'[41] Despite the opinion of Hitler, as Cesarani elaborates further, whether they were members of the Jewish community or were not associated with it, German Jews were indistinguishable from other Germans.[42]

The opinion of Hitler, as articulated in Mein Kampf, seems to dismiss this idea of integration or a shared sense of being German. This is an opinion that will be considered

---

36 David Cesarani, Final Solution, The Fate of The Jews 1933–49, (London: 2016), p. 7
37 *ibid,* p. 7
38 *ibid,* p. 7
39 *ibid,* p. 7
40 Adolf Hitler, Mein Kampf, p. 258
41 *ibid,* pp. 258–259
42 David Cesarani, Final Solution, p. 7

later with regards to modern attitudes to minority populations. Hitler suggested that: 'Germanisation can only be applied to *soil* and never to *people*.[43]

In parallels with modern society and negative attitudes towards immigrant or religious minority populations, there were some demographic, geographic, social and economic discrepancies that enabled Judeophobes to single Jews out. Cesarani notes that whilst half of the German population lived in small towns and villages, over two thirds of Jews lived in cities.[44] In fact, a third of the entire Jewish population (144,000) lived in Berlin, making up 4 per cent of the city's population; and in Berlin, as in other cities, there were some residential areas that were densely populated by Jews.[45] These areas were prosperous with the average Jewish household income being three times that of the average German family. There were significant numbers of poor Jews, but the majority of Jews were comfortably middle class.[46]

Further similarity to contemporary attitudes towards migrants and religious or other minorities, is the perception and treatment of the most concentrated and noticeable segment of the Jewish population, the Ostjuden. These migrants from the east compromised a quarter of the Jewish residents of Berlin, and outnumbered German born Jews in Leipzig and Dresden. The Ostjuden did not have German citizenship, they spoke Yiddish, and were religiously Orthodox, although, as Cesarani observes, and in another contemporary parallel, their children rapidly assimilated

---

43 Adolf Hitler, Mein Kampf, p. 353
44 David Cesarani, Final Solution, p. 7
45 *ibid*, p. 7
46 *ibid*, p. 7

into mainstream society.[47] The Ostjuden lived in the more rundown inner-city areas, and large numbers, due to their employment in artisan trades or manual labour, were hard hit by the Depression and had to rely on relief from Jewish charities. This caused some hostility from German Jews, who blamed them for rising levels of anti-Jewish feeling.[48]

Yet more similarity to modern attitudes can be observed in that, after the First World War, German federal and state authorities had tried to stop Jews from immigrating across the eastern border. The Prussian authorities rounded up and deported approximately 4,000 Jewish illegal immigrants between 1918 and 1921.[49] Attacks on the Ostjuden became more venomous after the Russian Revolution. Conservative and nationalist Germans had, for a long time, falsely accused eastern Jews of importing crime, vice, and disease; they now also accused them of spreading revolutionary ideas.[50]

Mein Kampf elaborates at length regarding Hitler's, and therefore National Socialism's anti-Semitism and hostility towards Jews. Hitler perceived Jews to be the great agitators for the destruction of Germany.[51] In language that is often mirrored by far-right and populist nationalist groups today, but contemporarily directed towards other targets, Hitler stated that: 'Wherever in the world we read of attacks against Germany, Jews are their fabricators, just as in peacetime and during the War the press of the Jewish stock-exchange and Marxists systematically stirred up

---

47 *ibid*, p. 8
48 *ibid*, p. 8
49 *ibid*, p. 8
50 *ibid*, p. 8
51 Adolf Hitler, Mein Kampf, p. 568

hatred against Germany until state after state abandoned neutrality and, renouncing the true interest of the peoples, entered the service of the world war coalition.'[52]

Hitler was fixated somewhat on the idea of the purity of the Aryan race and the Germanic peoples, suggesting that what was: '…universally valid in nature, is not only the sharp outward delimitation of the various races, but their uniform character in themselves.'[53] Elaborating on this theme, in a manner that also has contemporary parallels in the attitudes of modern nationalists, Hitler suggested that the higher purpose of what he referred to as the 'folkish state' was concern for the preservation of original racial elements. He believed that Aryans needed to conceive the state as a living organism of nationality.[54]

National Socialism did not confine its ideas of purity to Jews. As Richard Evans observes, even before the First World War ideas regarding eugenics and social Darwinism were having an impact on attitudes towards serious and violent offenders, and were being used in the legal profession, political life, and in the press as a means of justifying the death penalty.[55] After the defeat in the First World War, the idea of Nordic supremacy increased, along with a belief in the inferiority of Jews, Slavs and other races, which was adopted by greater numbers of racial hygiene specialists, with the medical model being applied to those identified as being politically deviant.[56] The crudeness of eugenics theory and

---

52 *ibid,* p. 568

53 *ibid,* p.259

54 *ibid,* p.358

55 Richard J. Evans, The Third Reich in History and Memory, (London: 2015), p. 74

56 *ibid,* p. 74

practice was demonstrated on 14 July 1933, when Hitler's cabinet approved the Law for the Prevention of Genetically Ill Offspring, thus legalising sterilisation on the grounds of racial hygiene.[57] In April 1933, in a further attempt to ostracise Jews, the National Socialist government sanctioned a boycott of Jewish businesses, lawyers and doctors.[58] Already a pattern of intolerance towards those deemed to be social unacceptable was being established. A letter from Reinhard Heydrich in September 1934 discussed how the imposition of strict laws was an incentive for Jews to leave Germany.[59] This too has some contemporary parallels in that modern populist nationalists and elements of the far-right will suggest that those who question or object to the laws of a nation state should leave, rather than seek changes in the law, and that if they have nowhere to go, they should go to the country of their racial, cultural, or religious heritage.

For those Jews who remained in Germany the legal situation became more difficult. The Nuremberg Race Laws of September 1935 sought to define Jewishness, forbade marriage and sexual relations between Jews and Aryans, and banned Jews from employing young Aryan women as domestic servants. The Reich Citizenship Law restricted citizenship to persons of German or kindred blood. In effect Jews were reduced to subjects with no political rights.[60] By 1937 Hitler was publically referring to Jews as 'inferior through and through,' and as 'the global peril.'[61] Public hostility towards Jews was gradually becoming normalised

---

57 Volker Ullrich, Hitler, (London: 2016), pp. 546–547
58 *ibid*, p. 441
59 *ibid*, p. 553
60 David Cesarani, Final Solution, p. 105
61 Volker Ullrich, Hitler, p. 658

and socially acceptable. One of many warnings from history is the normalising of hate, particularly when it is apparently sanctioned at multiple levels of society.

The Berlin Wannsee Conference in January 1942 set matters in motion for the Final Solution of the Jewish problem. The overall aim was that European Jews should be concentrated in the occupied eastern territories and murdered there, either straight away, or by working them to death.[62] Most Jews in the General Government in Poland in 1942 died in Belzec, Treblinka, and Sobibor, during Operation Reinhard. The Nazis also applied this term to the SS concentration camps at Auschwitz-Birkenau and Majdanek which operated simultaneously as extermination camps.[63] The camps at Belzec, Treblinka and Sobibor alone are estimated to have claimed about 1,500,000 lives in 1942.[64] The contempt for Jewish life is clearly demonstrated by the systematic slaughter in the camps, and is worthy of contemporary reflection in the attitudes to minorities expressed by some today. The disdain was equally apparent in the use of ghettoes such as Warsaw where 400,000 people were crammed into an area two and a half miles long and half a mile wide, from which they faced being shot on sight if they left, or trying to survive on starvation rations.[65] When the Jews did not die quickly enough Himmler ordered that they should be removed, and so from July to October 1942

---

62 Nicholas Wachsmann, KL: A History of the Nazi Concentration Camps, (London: 2013), p. 295
63 *ibid*, p. 295
64 *ibid*, p. 307
65 William I. Shirer, The Rise and Fall of the Third Reich, (London: 1960), p. 975

approximately 310,322 were transferred to Treblinka where they were gassed.[66]

As Robert Jan van Pelt observes, the significance of the Final Solution of the Jewish Problem was its state-initiated, state-sponsored, and state-controlled nature as a pro-gramme of genocide.[67] There is a general consensus among historians that the Germans killed between five million and possibly as many as six and a half million European Jews.[68] Van Pelt suggests that Raul Hilberg's estimate of the total number of Jewish deaths is the most reliable, and as such he opines that the Holocaust claimed 5.1 Million Jewish lives, of which, over 800,000 died due to ghettoization and general privation, 1.3 million were murdered in open-air shootings, and up to 3 million died in the camps. And of the camps, Auschwitz had the highest mortality with 1 million Jews, followed by Treblinka with 750,000 Jews and Belzec with 550,000 Jews.[69] Nicholas Wachsmann suggests that it can be estimated that 2.3 million men, women, and children were forced into SS concentration camps (excluding camps solely for extermination) between 1933 and 1945, and of these 1.7 million lost their lives.[70]

At Auschwitz, a camp central to the Nazi's plan for the extermination of European Jewry, some two hundred thousand Jews were selected on arrival for slave labour with other prisoners, whilst it is suggested by Wachsmann that 870,000 Jewish men, women, and children were selected for

---

66 *ibid,* p. 975

67 Robert Jan van Pelt, The Case for Auschwitz: Evidence from the Irving Trial, (Indiana: 2016), p. 12

68 *Ibid,* p. 12

69 *Ibid,* p. 6

70 Nicholas Wachsmann, KL, p. 6

immediate death in the gas chambers without ever being registered in the camp.[71] Elements of the far-right can seek to deny the totality of the Holocaust, and will refer to the numbers registered in Auschwitz, compared to the estimated deaths. As Wachsmann correctly observes–and this is supported by most historians–many, if not most of those who died in Auschwitz, were sent straight to their deaths without ever being registered.

These figures, as examples, emphasise the contempt that Nazis felt for Jews, and their willingness, through indoctrinated hatred, and a process of dehumanising an entire people, to attempt to eradicate the Jews of Europe by multiple means including shooting, gas chambers, slave labour, ghettoization, and deprivation of essential nourishment and medical treatment.

Alon Confino proposed that it is necessary to discuss the world that the Nazis and some Germans built or wanted– a Germany and later a world without Jews–and how they thought that they were engaged in a battle against their enemy, the Jew, and how memories, identities, fantasies and symbols are at the centre of their explanation.[72] It could be suggested that seeking to explain or rationalise can be seen as part of the denial process identified by Gregory H. Stanton in his Ten Stages of Genocide described earlier in this book.[73] Confino suggests that the notion of the radicalisation of racial ideology has been a factor in capturing the contingency that ran through the making of

---

71 *Ibid*, p. 6
72 Alon Confino, Reflections. A world Without Jews: Interpreting the Holocaust, German History, Vol 27, 4 (2009), p. 532
73 Gregory H. Stanton, Genocide Watch

the Holocaust.[74] Confino cites Ian Kershaw (Ian Kershaw, The Nazi Dictatorship) in proposing that no single decision brought about the Final Solution, but that: 'a lengthy process of radicalization in the search for 'a solution to the Jewish Question' between spring 1941 and summer 1942—as part of an immense overall resettlement and 'ethnic cleansing' programme for central and eastern Europe, vitiated through the failure to defeat the Soviet Union in 1941—was punctuated by several phases of sharp escalation.'[75]

This book in part discusses tribalism and hate. Confino opines that plans for deportation and extermination, particularly as part of the General Plan for the East, were never limited to the Jews, but also involved Poles, Russians, and Gypsies–in effect entire populations.[76] It is suggested that perhaps the central innovation of Holocaust scholarship over the last generation has been the emphasis on racial ideology, whereas previously, the motivations for the Nazis were seen as emanating from anti-Semitic beliefs, with the Holocaust at the centre of the Nazi regime's overall racial ideology.[77] Citing other studies, Confino suggests that those who carried out the extermination were committed ideologues who wanted to build a better world through genocide.[78]

In considering the concept of tribalism and populist nationalism in the context of the Nazis, Confino suggests that vast scholarship shows that the racial ideology of the Nazi regime: 'penetrated well beyond this circle of Nazi true

---

74 Alon Confino, Reflections. A World Without Jews, p. 535
75 *ibid*, p. 535
76 *ibid*, pp. 535–536
77 *ibid*, pp. 535–536
78 *ibid*, pp. 535–536

believers into all levels of society, be it institutions (the army or the churches), social spheres (cinema, architecture, or sport), or cultural artefacts (ranging from children's board games to the Nuremberg Party rallies).'[79] Elaborating on this theme he suggests that a combination of the notions of racial ideology, taken in context of war, and Nazi radicalisation, all constituted the: 'dominant interpretive framework for understanding the Holocaust, a framework that allowed for different interpretative configurations.'[80] It is proposed by Confino that the historiography of the last three decades has conclusively shown that Nazism's novelty was its attempt to create a society based on racial and biological ideas.[81]

Continuing the discussion of National Socialist racism and anti-Semitism, for comparison with contemporary attitudes of intolerance, Confino convincingly obseerves that historiography has shown that race penetrated every aspect of life in Nazi Germany, including those aspects which, for decades, seemed wholly unrevealing about that period of history. Racial ideology was behind the Nazi pursuit of happiness, and it is suggested that Hitler's wish to promote a sense of wellbeing was realised through: 'racism, an excessive war, plundering, and extermination.'[82]

In a further comparison to modern intolerance towards racial, religious and other minorities it is notable that Nazi ideology perceived: 'the Jews as the harbingers of modern evils, of communism, capitalism, liberalism, atheism, as well as being the culprits for the German recent past.'[83]

---

79 *ibid*, pp. 535–536
80 *ibid*, pp. 535–536
81 *ibid*, pp. 535–536
82 *ibid*, pp. 540–541
83 *ibid*, pp. 551–552

As Confino elaborates, in discussing the use of symbolism against Jews: 'these rituals of degradation spoke the rhetoric of racial ideology but used the symbols of past relationships between Jews and Christians.'[84] It does not take any stretch of imagination to see how modern political discourse and the language of far-right groups also seeks to use some historical rationale of religious Christian duty as a justification for words and actions that may cause harm or distress. This theme will be discussed later.

---

84 *ibid,* pp. 551–552

BOSNIA AND SREBRENICA

The continent of Europe had been lulled into a sense of security in the years following the Second World War. The conflicts that had brought so much destruction seemed to be in the past, and even the Cold War had not spilled over into bloodshed. This changed following the break-up of Yugoslavia and the brutality of the ensuing civil war. Why Yugoslavia descended into such conflict is open to debate. Rory J. Conces observes that the simplistic version often given is that ancient hatreds were part of the Balkan way of life.[85] Such an opinion presupposes that following the death of Tito, hitherto the source of stability and cohesion, the people of Yugoslavia reverted back to their tradition of ethnic and religious hatred and fighting.[86] However Conces observes that this view is a grand deception and: 'a myth which was carefully propagated by those who caused the conflict' as well as a failure to understand Bosnian history by those who accepted such an explanation.[87] It is suggested

---

85 Rory J. Conces, A Sisyphean Tale: The Pathology of Ethnic Nationalism and the Pedagogy of Forging Humane Democracies in the Balkans, *Studies in East European Thought*, 57 (2005), pp. 139–140

86 *ibid*, pp. 139–140

87 *ibid*, pp. 139–140

that whilst Balkan history has not always been peaceful it has actually not been any more turbulent that many other regions in Europe, and there is a need to look beyond the idea of age-old antagonisms.[88] Conces proposes that the events which swept the region occurred in large part because of a few political leaders: 'promoting their grand economic and political plans through the lens of ethnic nationalism with its xenophobia and chauvinism.'[89]

As Marko Attila Hoare observes, the atrocities in former Yugoslavia and Rwanda have increased the scholarly interest in the phenomena of genocide, ethnic cleansing, and mass murder, with discussions in comparative studies giving prominence to former Yugoslavia. However, scholars are divided over the extent to which the atrocities in former Yugoslavia can be classed as genocide.[90] Ivan Zverzhanovski suggests that the Yugoslav war was a clash of state making projects and that foremost among these was the Serbian project designed to re-draw the territorial boundaries left by the dissolving of the Socialist Federative Republic of Yugoslavia, with the intention of creating an almost ethnically pure territory for Serbs.[91] Zverzhanovski, notes that the: 'scale, range and consistency of the methods used to terrorize the non-Serb populations of many different areas in Croatia, Bosnia and Kosovo did not and could not have

---

88 *ibid*, pp. 139–140

89 *ibid*, pp. 139–141

90 Marko Attila Hoare, Genocide in the Former Yugoslavia Before and After Communism, *EUROPE-ASIA STUDIES*, 62 (7) (September 2010), p. 1194

91 Ivan Zverzhanovski, Watching War Crimes: The Srebrenica Video and the Serbian Attitudes to the 1995 Srebrenica Massacre, *Southeast European and Black Sea Studies*, 7 (3) (September 2007), pp. 418–419

resulted from a spontaneous eruption of local resentment,' and adds that the objective was to remove all prospect for opposition through the use of terror applied for strategic purposes, with the main elements being provocation, take-over, use of force, mass detention in prison camps, and elimination through expulsion and execution.[92] Zverzhanovski rightly concludes that the commission of war crimes and crimes against humanity in former Yugoslavia was on a scale unseen in Europe since the end of the Second World War.[93]

Hoare refers to the genocidal treatment of the Muslim population of Bosnia during the first months of the war.[94] He suggests that the ethnic cleansing and mass murder in former Yugoslavia was genocide, but against Kosovars as well as against Muslims.[95] Conversely Hoare notes that some other scholars challenge the notion that it was a genocide. He cites Michael Mann (Mann 2005, p. 358) who observed that: 'I would not term Yugoslav cleansings in general as genocide. They were wild—with perpetrators sometimes out of control (not in Srebrenica), and with great local variations in their practices. It was not like the 'Final Solution.'"[96] However, Hoare chooses to use the term genocide in relation to crimes where there is a strong existing basis in both scholarly literature and in judicial verdicts.[97] For clarification he states that this refers to the 1940s Nazi genocide of Jews, Gypsies and others; the Ustasa genocide of Serbs, Jews and

---

92 *ibid*, pp. 418–419

93 *ibid*, p. 417

94 Marko Attila Hoare, Genocide in the Former Yugoslavia Before and After Communism, p. 1194

95 *ibid*, p. 1194

96 *ibid*, p. 1194

97 *ibid*, p. 1194

Gypsies; and the Chetnik genocide of Muslims and Croats. Hoare states that for the 1990s he means above all the Serb genocide of non-Serbs on Bosnia and Herzegovina.[98]

Some scholars may disagree regarding the scope of the genocide but, as Marko Milanovic observes, the International Court of Justice (ICJ) judged that Serbia was responsible under the Genocide Convention for failing to prevent the genocide committed by the Bosnian Serb Army in the Bosnian Town of Srebrenica in July 1995.[99] The ICJ also ruled that the only crime committed during the Bosnian War which amounted to genocide was the Srebrenica massacre. However the ICJ found that Serbia was neither directly responsible for the Srebrenica genocide, and neither was it complicit in it.[100] The verdict of the ICJ is inconsistent in some levels in that it found that whilst Serbia was not guilty of genocide or complicity in genocide, it was guilty of failing to prevent genocide due to its failure to prevent the actions of Bosnian Serb forces, specifically at Srebrenica.[101] The Srebrenica massacre is the worst atrocity on European soil since the end of the Second World War. Bosnian Serb forces, backed by paramilitary and police units, expelled women and girls while separating men and boys from their families. There followed an organised massacre of over 7,000 Muslim men and boys.[102] A further example of the crimes committed was the incidences of organised and sys-

---

98 *ibid*, p. 1194

99 Marko Milanovic, State Responsibility for Genocide: A Follow Up, *The European Journal of International Law*, 18 (4) (2007), pp 669–670

100 *ibid*, pp. 669–670

101 Marko Attila Hoare, Genocide in the Former Yugoslavia Before and After Communism, p. 1195

102 Ivan Zverzhanovski, Watching War Crimes, pp. 417–418

tematic rape with the intention of forced pregnancy as an objective of the Serbs. Rape was seen as having a specific and strategic military purpose, with rape and other abuses designed to drive the non-Serbian population away.[103]

As Hoare observes, there are issues about how genocide in Bosnia and elsewhere during the Yugoslav civil war is defined. The ICJ accepted that systematic and large-scale mass killings of Bosnian Muslims had occurred across Bosnia in 1992, but the court ruled that these acts could not be considered genocide unless there was conclusive proof that there had been a specific aim to destroy the Bosnian Muslim population in whole or in part.[104] However, the court was satisfied that there was such an intent at Srebrenica, but there is a debate about why systematic mass killings in one area are deemed to be genocide and in other areas are perceived as ethnic cleansing; which, as Hoare notes, is the same as genocide apart from in motive.[105] This leads the discussion onto how war crimes and genocide have been dealt with legally, specifically regarding the Nazi regime and the atrocities in former Yugoslavia.

---

103 *ibid,* p. 419
104 Marko Attila Hoare, Genocide in the Former Yugoslavia
    Before and After Communism, p. 1210
105 *ibid,* p. 1210

War Crimes Trials– Nuremberg and Bosnia

Between 1945 and 1949, approximately 207 former Nazis were indicted and tried for war crimes and crimes against humanity in what has become known as The Nuremberg Trials.[106] Although the term 'genocide' had been articulated before the trials it was not fully employed within the trial process by the prosecutors.[107] The trials of the SS-Einsatzgruppen between 1947 and 1948 focussed on twenty-two high ranking SS officers who were tried for crimes against humanity.[108] It is estimated that the SS-Einsatzgruppen killed one million civilians (mainly Jews), between June 1941 and July 1943, which was clear evidence of genocide according to Lemkin's definition.[109]

Surprisingly the Holocaust did not play a leading role in the Nuremberg trials. It was of course a factor but was somewhat placed with other war crimes and atrocities which the

---

106 Hilary Earl, Prosecuting Genocide Before the Genocide Convention: Raphael Lemkin and the Nuremberg Trials, 1945–1949, *Journal of Genocide Research*, 15 (3) (2013), p. 317

107 *ibid*, p. 317

108 *ibid*, p. 317

109 *ibid*, p. 317

United States Chief Prosecutor Robert Jackson saw as peripheral to the main issue, which was that of the Nazi designed and illegal attack on international peace.[110] Jackson saw the atrocities as being preparatory or done in the execution of what he saw as the main crime.[111] As McGuiness notes, Jackson reported that: 'the reason that this program of extermination of Jews and destruction of the rights of minorities becomes an international concern is this: it was part and a plan for making an illegal war. Unless we have a war connection as a basis for reaching them, I would think we have no basis for dealing with atrocities.'[112] For the British too, the Holocaust and other crimes were seen to be very important but a secondary reason for punishment.[113] The USSR had moved swiftly to try the Germans for crimes in the areas that the Soviets reoccupied from late 1943 to early 1944, but later agreed to United States plans for Nuremberg. Later the Soviets used the trials for propaganda purposes.[114] It is apparent that there were difficulties in marrying the aims and objectives of the International Military Tribunal and trials at Nuremberg with the subsequent goals of the Universal Declaration of Human Rights. Inconsistencies in the enforcement of human rights, war crimes trials, and the punishment of the crime of genocide have proved to be an ongoing issue.

The first of the thirteen Nuremberg Trials was the International Military Tribunal (IMT) at which the allied powers of the U.S, Britain, France, and the Soviet Union prosecuted twenty-two (twenty-three including Martin Bormann

---

110Margaret E. McGuinness, Peace v. Justice, p. 755

111 *ibid*, p. 755

112*ibid, p.* 755

113*ibid, p.* 755

114*ibid, p.* 755

tried in absentia) high ranking Nazis. These were followed by indictments and prosecutions in twelve Subsequent Nuremberg Trials or NMT.[115] The SS-Einsatzgruppen Trial between 29 September 1947 and 10 April 1948 was the first war crimes trial to deal with individuals whose sole role was their participation in the genocidal murder of Jews; thus making it significant in the history and prosecution of genocide in international law.[116] As Hilary Earl observes, the SS-Einsatzgruppen were the vanguard of the Final Solution, and were deployed in the Soviet Union in the summer of 1941 to kill those who were seen as racial and political enemies of the Third Reich.[117] Between 1941 and 1943, four divisions of SS-Einsatzgruppen (approximately 3000 men), assisted by the German army and other reinforcements, murdered approximately one million Soviet civilians–mainly Jews–including Roma, the mentally ill, and Soviet commissars.[118] This conformed to Lemkin's definition of genocide which described genocide as the 'destruction of the nation or an ethnic group' (including culturally).[119] At the IMT the U.S Prosecutor, Jackson, did include genocide in Count Three of the indictment for war crimes:

(A) MURDER AND ILL-TREATMENT OF CIVILIAN POPULATIONS…
…murders and ill-treatment were carried out by diverse means, including shooting, hanging,

---

115Hilary Earl, Prosecuting Genocide Before the Genocide Convention, p. 318

116*ibid,* p. 318

117*ibid,* p. 318

118*ibid,* p. 318

119*ibid,* p. 318

gassing, starvation, gross overcrowding…and torture of all kinds…They conducted deliberate and systematic genocide, viz., the extermination of racial and national groups, against the civilian populations…of occupied territories in order to destroy particular races and classes of people and national, racial, or religious groups, particularly Jews, Poles, and Gypsies and others.[120]

This at least allowed for a broader scope of prosecution and indicated the intent of the Nazi regime which had made clear its desire to eradicate European Jewry. Indeed, as Earl observes: 'Nazi racial theory targeted Jews and Bolsheviks as enemies of the state, the units of the SS–Einsatzgruppen had killed approximately one million individuals from the targeted groups, therefore, the intention had always been to 'exterminate' them.'[121] One failure of the Nuremberg Trials was that it did not address the peacetime crimes of the Holocaust.[122] This led Raphael Lemkin to use the new General Assembly to find a way to criminalise genocide–the term he had coined to describe a state's elimination or attempt to eliminate, an entire people. The Genocide Convention was adopted in December 1948, two days before the Universal Declaration of Human Rights.[123] If good had come from the horrors of Nazi atrocities and the Holocaust, it was that the international community

---

120 *ibid,* pp. 322–323

121 *ibid,* p. 331

122 Margaret E. McGuinness, Peace v. Justice: The Universal Declaration of Human Rights and the Modern Origins of the Debate, *Diplomatic History,* 35 (5) (2011), p. 755

123 *ibid,* p. 755

acknowledged this new definition of a specific war crime, and accepted the need to protect as sacrosanct, the human rights of civilians.

Europe and the international community had to revisit the concept of war crimes due to the atrocities of the war following the break-up of Yugoslavia. The United Nations (UN) Commission of Experts, established following a UN Security Council Resolution on 6 October 1992, sought to investigate allegations of breaches of the Geneva Conventions and other violations of international humanitarian law in the former territory of Yugoslavia, and concluded that Serb war crimes encompassed genocide.[124] The Commission's interim report of 9 February 1993 noted that ethnic cleansing had been carried out:

> …by means of murder, torture, arbitrary arrest and detention, extra-judicial executions, rape and sexual assaults, confinement of civilian population in ghetto areas, forcible removal, displacement and deportation of civilian population, deliberate military attacks or threats of attacks on civilians and civilian areas, and wanton destruction of property. Those practices constitute crimes against humanity and can be assimilated to specific war crimes. Furthermore, such acts could also fall within the meaning of the Genocide Convention.[125]

The Bosnians argued that the totality of the crimes committed by Bosnian Serbs during the conflict amounted

---

124 Marko Attila Hoare, Genocide in the Former Yugoslavia Before and After Communism, pp. 1206–1207
125 *ibid,* pp. 1206–1207

to genocide, particularly the massacre at Srebrenica, the siege of Sarajevo, and the atrocities in the Prijedor area and prison camps.[126] The Bosnian strategy hoped to improve the potential outcome of the case for their citizens and politicians as they would struggle to explain how those who died at Srebrenica were victims of genocide, whilst those who died at Sarajevo were not.[127] However, the International Court of Justice (ICJ) was unable to find a reason why a pattern of crimes against humanity should be treated as a single crime of genocide without proof of a clear plan.[128]

One needs to consider intent, act, or omission with complicity to commit genocide. The International Criminal Tribunal for Rwanda (ICTR) Appeals chamber stated that it considered aiding and abetting to be part of complicity in genocide.[129] As Milanovic observes, factors such as instigation might require the presence of genocidal intent, but aiding and abetting does not.[130] Complicity can be seen as a general term for various parts of participation in criminal behaviour; whereas *mens rea* depends on the specific type of complicity. Milanovic gives as a good example the unscrupulous businessman selling poison to Auschwitz. He will certainly be aware that the camp has a genocidal purpose, but he is not necessarily an accomplice to genocide; however, he is still acting deliberately if he knows what the gas will be used for but is indifferent to the consequences.[131] From

---

126 *ibid*, pp. 1206–1207
127 Marko Milanovic, State Responsibility for Genocide: A Follow Up, p. 672
128 *ibid*, p. 672
129 *ibid*, pp. 682–683
130 *ibid*, pp. 682–683
131 *ibid*, pp. 682–683

this it is taken that aiding and abetting genocide is always deliberate, even if it is not done so with specific intent–it is not an act of negligence.[132] This is of relevance with all genocides, and, as will be considered later, it requires consideration with the language and rhetoric of hate that may have harmful consequences.

It is clear that states have a duty to prevent genocide within their own territory, but, as Milanovic notes, it is less clear what the national and international obligations are regarding genocide in other lands.[133]

The ICJ observed, with regard to state obligation to prevent genocide:

A State does not incur responsibility simply because the desired result is not achieved; responsibility is however incurred if the State manifestly failed to take all measures to prevent genocide which were within its power, and which might have contributed to preventing the genocide. In this area the notion of 'due diligence', which calls for an assessment *in concreto,* is of critical importance. Various parameters operate when assessing whether a State has duly discharged the obligation concerned. The first, which varies greatly from one State to another, is clearly the capacity to influence effectively the action of persons likely to commit, or already committing, genocide.

This capacity itself depends, among other things, on the geographical distance of the state concerned from the scene of the events, and on the strength of

---

132 *ibid,* p. 683
133 *ibid,* p. 685

the political links, as well as links of all other kinds, between the authorities of that State and the main actors in the events. The State's capacity to influence must also be assessed by legal criteria, since it is clear that every State may only act within the limits permitted by international law; seen thus, a State's capacity to influence may vary depending on its particular legal position vis-à-vis the situations and persons facing the danger, or the reality, of genocide.[134]

This specifies that there is an international obligation to intervene and take action to prevent genocide, and this does not require an individual state to have jurisdiction over a person, a group of individuals, or a territory. Such international standards have arisen from the experience of genocides after they have occurred. If there is a responsibility to act nationally and within nation states to prevent the extremes of genocide, then there must also be obligations to prevent matters reaching that stage.

---

134 *ibid*, p. 685

Tribalism, Discrimination, Prejudice, and Racism

Is tribalism normal? On balance of probability it would be reasonable to suggest that most examples of tribalism are healthy, useful, and benign. They ensure that social groups–family, local, regional, national, sporting, employment etc.–work together for the common good. Tribal communities, however they may be defined, cooperate with others, maintain various levels of security, uphold law and order, protect and cultivate resources, share a bond of commonality, trade with different groups, form allegiances in times of shared struggle, care for the old, the young, and the sick, and form means of protection during periods of danger and threat. Indeed, the forming of intergroup relationships also ensures the continuation of a healthy bloodline without the genetic risks associated with incestuous inbreeding. Yet history is marked by episodes where tribalism has contributed to hostility, violence, war, and genocide. Part of the reason may be prejudice based on the perception of others as an 'out-group' that are considered to be a danger to the 'in-group' even if there is no clear evidence or reason to fear such danger.

Marilynn B. Brewer, referring in part to the work of Gordon Allport (1954), recognised that attachment to an 'in-group' does not necessarily require hostility toward 'out-groups.'[135] Yet, as Brewer observes, the approach to studies of ethnocentrism and what is referred to as 'in-group bias' presumes that love for that group and hate for the 'out-group' are reciprocally related.' [136] Laboratory experiments and cross-cultural research suggest that 'in-group' identification and negative attitudes towards 'out-groups' is independent and may be motivated by preferential treatment of 'in-group' members rather than direct hostility towards the 'out-group.'[137] Brewer cites Allport in stating that:

> Although we could not perceive our own in-groups excepting as they contrast to out-groups, still the in-groups are psychologically primary.... Hostility toward out-groups helps strengthen our sense of belonging, but it is not required.... The familiar is preferred. What is alien is regarded as somehow inferior, less "good," but there is not necessarily hostility against it.... Thus, while a certain amount of predilection is inevitable in all in-group memberships, the reciprocal attitude toward out-groups may range widely.[138]

Lasana T. Harris and Susan T. Fiske suggest that: 'Laypeople characterize prejudice broadly as general animosity toward another person or social group. Researchers

---

135 Marilynn B. Brewer, The Psychology of Prejudice: Ingroup Love or Outgroup Hate, *Journal of Social Issues*, 55 (3) (1999), pp. 429–430
136 *ibid*, pp. 429–430
137 *ibid*, pp. 429–430
138 *ibid*, pp. 429–430

themselves have traditionally viewed prejudice simply as dislike of an individual primarily because of his or her perceived membership in a social group.'[139] Gordon Allport in 1954 described prejudice somewhat broadly as an antipathy based on a perceived social category.[140] Harris and Fiske, using neuroimaging and neuroscience data, suggest that there are indications that extreme forms of prejudice may deny their targets even full humanity.[141] Dehumanising 'the other' has been an observable factor in genocides as cited earlier in the Ten Stages of Genocide compiled by Gregory H.Stanton.[142]

It is suggested that to understand the roots of prejudice and discrimination requires a better understanding of what 'in-group' identification and formation serves as a purpose for human beings.[143] Brewer, again citing Allport, opines that the familiar is preferred, and that what is alien can be regarded as inferior or less good, but not necessarily with hostility against it. As such attitudes towards 'out-groups' may vary widely.[144] In considering the extremes of tribalism, prejudice and hate that lead to harm it is noted by Brewer that moral superiority, combined with fear and distrust of 'out-groups, with added social comparison, are all processes that arise from what she refers to as 'in-group maintenance.' Brewer adds that favouritism can lead to conflict between groups even when realistic conflict over material resources

---

139 Lasana T. Harris and Susan T. Fiske, Dehumanising the Lowest of the Low: Neuroimaging Responses to Extreme Out-Groups, *Psychological Science,* 17 (10) (2006), p. 847
140 *ibid,* p. 847
141 *ibid,* p. 847
142 Gregory H. Stanton, Genocide Watch
143 Marilynn B. Brewer, The Psychology of Prejudice, pp. 429–430
144 *ibid,* pp. 429–430

and power is absent.[145] This is relevant when considering the hostility to minority racial or religious groups when there is no obvious or logical reason to perceive a danger from the entirety of such groups, or when animosity is disproportionate to any factor that may have led to it.

Brewer elaborates on this point by noting that when groups are political entities, these processes of prejudice may be exacerbated through deliberate manipulation by group leaders in order to mobilise collective action to secure or maintain political power.[146] Leaders of political groups with electoral potential, and of protest groups that agitate populist nationalism, all have the potential to manipulate in this way. As Brewer observes, social differentiation can provide fault lines in any social system that can be exploited for political purposes, and that when trust is 'in-group' based it is easier to fear control by outsiders, with perceived common threat being a unifier of 'in-group' cohesion.[147]

Research from Canada, based on data from several countries, showed that feelings of threat to well-being due to poor economic conditions, were positively related to negative attitudes to towards primary immigrant groups.[148] In an observation that would apply internationally it was noted that experimental evidence revealed that the manipulation of realistic threats posed by immigrants–in this case telling

---

145 *ibid,* pp. 437–438

146 *ibid,* pp. 437–438

147 *ibid,* pp. 437–438

148 Lisa Legault and Isabelle Green-Demers, The Protective Role of Self-Determined Prejudice Regulation in The Relationship Between Ingroup Threat and Prejudice, *Motivation & Emotion,* 36 (2012), pp. 144–145

Canadians that immigrants were taking Canadian jobs–increased negative attitudes towards them.[149]

Legault and Green-Demers note that a second domain of intergroup threat–symbolic threat–has been put forward to supplement the realistic conflict perspective. Symbolic threat refers to the perception of intergroup conflict in values, attitudes, morals and beliefs, rather than conflict due to competition and goals. Essentially they propose that symbolic threats include a perception by the 'in-group' that includes an imagined threat posed by the culture and values of the 'out-group'.[150] It is proposed that modern theories of prejudice, including modern, symbolic, and aversive racism are based on the symbolic threat perspective, and that the perception of challenged ideology differs from group conflict theory in that it is seen as a conflict over values rather than over resources. It is further noted that correlational and experimental studies have shown that symbolic threats are positively related to prejudice.[151] This too is relevant to contemporary discourse and political rhetoric in that the symbolic or perceived threat of danger from migrants, refugees, or minority groups does not necessarily correlate with the actual risk of harm or of negative impacts upon societies. Yet such a view is rarely challenged as it does not fit into the need of those who seek to demonise or dehumanise those perceived as being from outside of the 'in-group'.

As Brewer observes, many discriminatory perceptions and behaviours are primarily motivated by a desire to promote and to maintain positive relationships within the 'in-group' rather than due to antagonism towards perceived

---

149 *ibid*, pp. 144–145
150 *ibid*, pp. 144–145
151 *ibid*, pp. 144–145

'out-groups', and as such 'in-group' love does not automatically lead to 'out-group' hate.[152] However, 'in-group' attachment can lead to antagonism and distrust of those outside of the group and promote a need to justify values in the form of moral superiority and sensitivity to threat, with identification loyalty becoming marked by disdain and hostility to those outside of the group.[153] Brewer suggests that such forces are more likely to be powerful in highly segmented and hierarchically organised societies, whereas in societies characterised by multiple 'cross-cutting' group divisions it is less likely that 'in-group' loyalties will lead to antagonism towards 'out-groups'.[154]

Research using neuroimaging by Harris and Fiske refers to a Stereotype Content Model (SCM) which shows that some prejudice is worse. The SCM predicts that out-groups that are stereotypically hostile and incompetent such as addicts and the homeless, will be dehumanised.[155] The research states that the Medial Prefrontal Cortex (mPFC) is necessary for social cognition, and they examined functional magnetic resonance imaging to obtain data by viewing the brain activations of 10 participants viewing 48 photographs of social groups, and 12 participants viewing objects; with each picture representing one SCM quadrant.[156] Their analysis revealed mPFC activation to all social groups except extreme 'out-groups' who, it was noted,

---

152 Marilynn B. Brewer, The Psychology of Prejudice, pp. 441–442

153 *ibid*, pp. 441–442

154 *ibid*, pp. 441–442

155 Lasana T. Harris and Susan T. Fiske, Dehumanising the Lowest of the Low, p. 847

156 *ibid*, p. 847

activated insula and amygdala in a pattern consistent with disgust, which was the emotion predicted by the SCM.[157]

Objects rated with the same emotions did not activate the mPFC, which, it is suggested, provides neural evidence supporting the prediction that extreme 'out-groups' may be seen as less than human, or may be dehumanised.[158] Harris and Fiske note that not all groups provoke animosity. They suggest that groups stereotyped as competent and warm, such as the middle-class, elicited 'in-group' emotions of pride and admiration; whereas 'out-group' prejudices occurred in those who elicit envy, pity, and disgust.[159] Groups stereotyped as neither warm nor competent elicited the worst kind of prejudice–disgust and contempt–which was based on perceived moral violations and subsequent negative outcomes that these groups were alleged to have brought upon themselves.[160] This would fit in with some of the hostility directed towards groups such as the homeless, substance abusers, criminals, and also refugees who flee from war in their country of origin. As Harris and Fiske observe, extreme discrimination reveals the worst kind of prejudice and excludes all 'out-groups' from full humanity; and they note that modern accounts show how the target can be seen as less than a human being, and sometimes even an animal or an object.[161] This of course concurs with some of the language of hate and intolerance that dehumanises the target individuals or groups with generic and dismissive terms.

---

157 *ibid*, p. 847

158 *ibid*, p. 847

159 *ibid*, p. 847

160 *ibid*, pp. 847–848

161 *ibid*, p. 848

According to Harris and Fiske the SCM uniquely captures dehumanising prejudice, with target groups not being seen as fully human, but evidence that the lowest 'out-groups' are categorised as less than human remains elusive. They accept that this field of research lacks data that goes beyond self-reporting which is vulnerable to social desirability bias.[162] It should also be noted that the study by Harris and Fiske was based on a small sample. However, Harris and Fiske assert that the results empirically support the idea of dehumanisation and are consistent with verbal reports, insofar as neural evidence goes beyond verbal reports which may be subject to concerns of self-presentation.[163] They suggest further that such evidence, if replicated and extended, could help to explain the human potential to commit atrocities, hate crime, prisoner abuse, and genocide against those groups who have been dehumanised.[164]

The work of Harris and Fiske alludes to biological responses that may occur as indicators of prejudice, but they do not explain why such prejudice occurs. Derek Hook opines that understanding racism is theoretical and political. He suggests that it is theoretical in so much as it is a complex and over-determined set of phenomena that cannot easily succumb to easy, or intuitive conceptualisation.[165] It is political in as much as racism cannot properly be managed if society does not understand what sustains it and what supports its most visceral aspects.[166]

---

162 *ibid,* p. 848

163 *ibid,* p. 852

164 *ibid,* p. 848

165 Derek Hook, Pre Discursive Racism, *Journal of Community & Applied Social Psychology,* 16 (2006), p. 209

166 *ibid,* p. 209

Hook suggests that in seeking to combat racism, if the analysis is wrong it is likely that political strategy will not achieve any intended objectives.[167] He observes that: '... racism takes on a moral character, a near metaphysical quality: the 'racial other' and all their assumed attributes come to represent a series of cultural violations.'[168] Hook refers to the quasi-religious nature of racism such as in the case of anti-Semitism, in which the racial 'other' is not seen merely as being offensive in respect of their body, mind and culture, but is also seen as being repugnant because of the positive assault that they represent to the moral order of the world of the racist.[169]

Racial prejudice research has been dominated by an Anglo-centric perspective, particularly examining the attitudes of white Americans towards black Americans.[170] Confirming some earlier points in this book such research reveals that the pervasiveness and significant prevalence of explicit and implicit 'out-group' prejudice exists in majority group individuals and that such prejudice is very pervasive to minority group individuals.[171] McGrane and White suggest that minority groups are also capable of possessing implicit and explicit prejudice.[172]

Research conducted in an Australian context found that Asian participants displayed significantly less implicit

---

167 *ibid*, p. 209

168 *ibid*, pp. 225–226

169 *ibid*, pp. 225–226

170 Joshua A. McGrane and Fiona A. White, Differences in Anglo and Asian Australians' Explicit and Implicit Prejudice and the Attenuation of their Implicit In-Group Bias, *Asian Journal of Social Psychology*, 10 (2007), p. 204

171 *ibid*, p. 204

172 *ibid*, p. 204

prejudice but significantly greater explicit prejudice than their Anglo counterparts.[173] The McGrane and White study was deemed to have provided further evidence of the dissociation of explicit and implicit attitudes, particularly in regard to their predication.[174] Additionally it was found that brief exposure to positive 'out-group' exemplars attenuated the implicit bias of Asian but not Anglo participants, which, it is suggested, showed that the technique may have been contingent upon more fundamental prejudice reducing measures, and that support to undermine implicit biases required a long-term process.[175] The research also suggested a critical need for positive depictions of Asians in Australian society.[176] This need for positive depictions of minority groups should apply to other societies.

It is proposed by Legault and Green-Demers that: 'the motivation to be non-prejudiced and intergroup threat interact in important ways, such that having self-determined motivation to be non-prejudiced absorbs the negative effects of threat, whereas non-self-determined prejudice regulation amplifies the impact of threat on prejudice.'[177] This would appear to suggest that prejudice and the perception of threat can be controlled through self-motivation. However, Legault and Green-Demers note that self-determined motivation alone does not provide any immunity to the feeling of intergroup threat or even, presumably, the feeling of threat itself, but it may absorb or provide a buffer to the negative

---

173 *ibid*, p. 204

174 *ibid*, p. 204

175 *ibid*, p. 204

176 *ibid*, p. 204

177 Lisa Legault and Isabelle Green-Demers, The Protective Role of Self-Determined Prejudice Regulation, p. 155

consequences of feeling threatened which includes prejudice.[178] This may suggest a factor that enhances the potential for intergroup tolerance and cooperation. As Legault and Green-Demers elaborate, most people will demonstrate concern and sensitivity to threatened or challenged 'in-group' security and values, as these challenges comprise a significant and tangible portion of intergroup relations.[179] Additionally, acknowledging challenge and threat will serve as an adaptive function.[180] However, with self-determined prejudice the regulators do not translate perceived threat into negative attitudes, but non-self-determined prejudice regulators do. This suggests that: 'individual difference lies in the reaction to (and regulation of) intergroup threat–with non-self-determined prejudice regulators reacting with more hostility.'[181] The differences in individual and group motivation to regulate prejudice–which must apply to government level as well–can have important socio-political implications.[182] The same study observed that Canada and the United States have high immigration rates per capita, which leads to challenges in incorporating immigrants and visible minorities into both the workforce and wider society. Legault and Green-Demers suggest–reasonably–that prejudice is linked to having non-self-determined or controlled regulation of bias, and that, pressuring students, workers or citizens to abide by external standards of political correctness may be counter-productive if the value of such standards is not emphasised.[183] This of

---

178 *ibid*, p. 155
179 *Ibid*, p. 155
180 *Ibid*, p. 155
181 *ibid*, p. 155
182 *ibid*, p. 156
183 *ibid*, p. 156

course may be of value for educators and those who make policies, as prejudice reduction requires support from the wide social environment of educators, parents, employers, social institutions, and government.[184]

The question is sometimes raised about whether there is a Nazi personality, which is somehow predisposed to the actions and crimes associated with National Socialism and similar regimes. The defendants at the Nuremberg Trial underwent psychological and psychiatric assessments. The material from those assessments, particularly the Rorschach inkblot tests, were the subject of a detailed review by Eric A. Zillmer, Molly Harrower, Barry A. Ritzier, and Robert P. Archer. Ritzier saw his first Rorschach record of a Nazi in 1970 as postdoctoral fellow at Yale Psychiatric Institute. The students were asked to review an unidentified Rorschach inkblot protocol, and only knew that it belonged to a famous person. The test that they reviewed was of Adolf Eichmann.[185] Eichmann had been portrayed by the media during his trial as a depraved killer responsible for the deaths of millions. The Rorschach did not show evidence of depravity, sadism, bigotry, hatred, or even an overwhelming sense of guilt. In fact the psychological profile of Eichmann appeared to: 'indicate an ordinary, rather untroubled person, who, although likely to be somewhat distant and inflexible in personal relationships, was not bent on the destruction of whole populations of human

---

184 *ibid,* p. 156

185 Eric A. Zillmer, Molly Harrower, Barry A. Ritzier, Robert P. Archer, The Quest for the Nazi Personality: A Psychological Investigation of Nazi War Criminals, (New York, Routledge, 2009), p. 8

beings.'[186] Eichmann's Rorschach protocol results made more sense to Zillmer *et al*, when they examined the work of Hannah Arendt who had been assigned to cover his 1961 trial in Jerusalem by *The New Yorker*.[187] After observing the trial and accessing interview information and psychological test data, Arendt proposed that the actions of Eichmann and other Nazis: 'were not related to significant psychological derangement in those men, but were a result of a lack of personality substance, that is, banality.'[188] Arendt suggested that Eichmann was neither a sadist, nor even an aggressive individual who had intent to cause harm to others for depraved satisfaction, but rather he was: 'just an ordinary, conscientious, moderately ambitious bureaucrat who was more interested in simply obeying orders than he was in sending millions of people to their deaths in the camps.'[189]

Zillmer *et al* reviewed Rorschach protocols of the senior Nazis from the Nuremberg Trial and also from rank-and-file Nazis and collaborators. They observed deficiencies in cognitive resources that are typically required for effective stress management.[190] They concluded that many of the Nazis may have had difficulties making their own decisions and were not high-level creative thinkers.[191] It was suggested that those individuals were vulnerable to becoming stressed out and potentially had a reduced capacity for stress tolerance.[192] These conclusions were reached whilst taking into

---

186 *ibid*, p. 9
187 *ibid*, pp. 9–10
188 *ibid*, *pp.* 9–10
189 *ibid*, pp. 9–10
190 *ibid*, *p.* 179
191 *ibid*, *p.* 179
192 *ibid*, *p.* 179

account potential situation variables associated with the war crimes trials. Yet it was observed that the Nazis who had been assessed had chronically low stress tolerance related to their insufficient personality resources for coping with stress. As such many of them needed the increased amount of structure, guidance and reassurance in their social and occupational lives which the Nazi structure may have given them.[193] It is argued that such individuals may have been particularly attracted to the quasi-military and rigid structure of the Nazi hierarchy which would include the idea of following orders.[194]

It would be simple to suggest that there is a homogeneous evil Nazi personality, but Zillmer *et al* suggest that their work was unsuccessful in finding one.[195] Furthermore they considered whether there are lawful relationships between psychopathology and a propensity for violence that could form a theoretical basis for the 'mad Nazi' theory.[196] Citing the work of Megargee (1984) they conclude that violence is not necessarily related to psychopathology, and state: 'Although a variety of functional and organic disturbances can lead to aggression and violent behaviour, most violence is committed by people suffering from no diagnosable impairment. Even if we exclude legal, socially condoned forms of violence such as warfare, we find criminal violence is often performed by normal people for rational motives.'[197]

The psychological and psychiatric assessments of the Nuremberg defendants and rank-and-file Nazis do not

---

193 *ibid, p.* 179
194 *ibid, p.* 179
195 *ibid,* p. 181
196 *ibid,* p. 183
197 *ibid,* p. 183

suggest madness or insanity as a factor in their allegiance to the Party, willingness to follow orders, or propensity for acts of extreme violence and involvement in genocide.

Hannah Arendt's report of the trial of Adolf Eichmann is subtitled: 'A Report on the Banality of Evil.'[198] There is no legal definition of evil and there is no clinical psychiatric or psychological diagnosis that specifies symptoms or characteristics. Evil is not something that is defined scientifically, but it is a concept, largely religious and social, that is understood. The 'banality of evil' adequately highlights the ordinariness of those who cause, or have the propensity to extreme harm. The susceptibility of ordinary people to the concept of an 'out-group' threat to the 'in-group' due to economic, symbolic, or cultural perceptions of that threat, is what should alert societies to potential risks of harm.

It is proposed in this book, and will be elaborated on further, that prejudice can be challenged by information, understanding, and positive acceptance. Integration of minority communities is essential, but that should not include forced assimilation with loss of cultural or religious identity, and integration should include overt acceptance by the majority community without this being seen as a threat to some form of established identity. Majority communities should be educated to understand the global nature of the world today, and also to recognise that large migrant waves are not just a passing reality, but also that such waves will, for reasons of familiarity and support, seek to group with others of a similar background (linguistic, cultural, religious) before fully joining and embracing wider society as citizens of the host community.

------

198 Hannah Arendt, Eichmann in Jerusalem: A Report on the Banality of Evil, (New York: 1977)

THE FAR-RIGHT AND POPULIST NATIONALISM

There appears to be an increase, or at least a consistent level, of far-right and populist nationalist sympathies and active political parties and protest groups. Some, as shall be shown, may fit a description of neo-Nazi or fascist based upon their politics and worldview; others may not be so obviously extreme but they have policies which sit well with more radical groups and which at times appear to cross over.

The United Kingdom Independence Party (UKIP) were formed with the purpose of ensuring that the UK left the European Union. Although UKIP would not claim to be an anti-Islam or anti-Muslim party, it has proposed a ban on the burqa and niqab, stating in the general election manifesto of 2017: 'UKIP will ban wearing of the niqab and the burqa in public places. Face coverings such as these are barriers to integration. We will not accept these dehumanising symbols of segregation and oppression, nor the security risks they pose.'[199] The manifesto does not specify what security risks these items of clothing pose, or why imposing a ban would

---

199 Anon, UKIP Manifesto 2017, www.ukip.org/manifesto2017, p. 37, accessed 15 August 2017

somehow liberate wearers from dehumanising segregation and oppression. Somewhat disingenuously the manifesto claims that there is no human right to conceal ones identity, and that the ban would help to liberate women by allowing them to be perceived as individuals in their own rights, it would promote communication and work opportunities, and in the ultimate attempt to deny any form of prejudice there is also a suggestion that the health of niqab and burqa wearers is a concern due to the lack of Vitamin D they do not receive from sunlight.[200]

The UKIP manifesto also suggested that female children deemed to be at risk of genital mutilation should be forced to undergo medical examinations (but targeting primarily those who are Muslim or who have a heritage that is not northern European). The manifesto claims that thousands of girls are failed by the Prohibition of Female Circumcision Act of 1985, and that UKIP, in an attempt to protect girls, would implement a screening programme for girls identified as being at risk of FGM (Female Genital Mutilation) from birth until the age of 16 which would consist of: 'annual non-invasive physical check-ups.' Girls seen to be at risk of FGM would also undergo checks on returning to the UK from trips abroad to countries where FGM is 'customary.'[201] Of course any physical examination of a child's genitals is by its very nature invasive, and if conducted without parental consent, would be assault, and possibly sexual assault. The proposal was made under the guise of child protection but no proposal was made for similar examinations of children not from those backgrounds who may be at risk of sexual abuse. It is therefore disingenuous

---

200 *ibid*, p. 37
201 *ibid*, p. 36

and seeks to emphasise the otherness of some within the UK community. In the area of sexual offences UKIP proposed that a higher sentence should be imposed if a crime is shown to have an aggravating factor of racial or religious motivation.[202]

Maintaining a theme linked to the Muslim community, UKIP proposed to address 'Islamist extremism' in prisons. The manifesto suggests segregation of extremists from the wider prison population, removal of better 'perks' for prisoners irrespective of faith (but in a section about addressing Islamist extremism), refusing admission to prisons of any imam, preacher or individual known to 'promote views contrary to British values' (without specifying what those values are), and giving prison governors new powers to combat Islamist extremism and gang violence in prisons.[203]There is a theme of defining the otherness of Muslims. It can be proposed that what the UKIP manifesto suggests is forced assimilation with the banning of clothing identifying a culture belonging to an 'out-group' and targeting that group for specific legislation to control, isolate or diminish any sense of cultural or religious heritage.

Part of the appeal of Hitler and the Nazis was that he and they were seen to be in touch with the men who had fought in the First World War. In a totally populist approach the 2017 UKIP election manifesto included a pledge that the party: 'will not allow veterans to be chased, harassed and intimidated by over-zealous human rights lawyers, most of whom are unlikely even to begin to comprehend the pressures of the battlefield.'[204] It was also proposed to

---

202 *ibid,* p. 41
203 *ibid,* p. 41
204 *ibid,* p. 46

introduce legislation preventing police and prosecutors from taking action against veterans for actions taken whilst in the service of the Crown, and that veterans will not be allowed to stand trial for: 'allegations of misconduct dating from half a century ago under any circumstances.'[205] The clear implication is of guaranteed amnesty after the fact, irrespective of evidence, and by suggestion, the granting of free rein to commit crime during active service. UKIP may be better defined as a populist nationalist party, but as shall be shown, there is a crossover in some areas that the party seeks to exploit and reach for wider appeal.

Are far-right groups fascist? The term has its origins in fascist Italy and has been applied to the National Socialism of Hitler's Germany.[206] Following the defeats of Mussolini's and Hitler's regimes, and with the rise of Marxist and totalitarian interpretations of fascism, a clearer definition became less obvious. The Cold War in particular, allowed inaccurate labelling to continue, and indeed, as Joachim Scholtyseck observes, the pessimism of George Orwell prevailed in that fascism had no meaning except that it signified something not desirable.[207] Emilio Gentile suggests that:

> …fascism is a modern political phenomenon, which is nationalistic and revolutionary, anti-liberal and anti-Marxist, organised in the form of a militia party, with a totalitarian conception of politics and

---

205 *ibid*, p. 46

206 Joachim Scholtyseck, Fascism—National Socialism—Arab "Fascism": Terminologies, Definitions and Distinctions, *Die Welt des Islams*, 52 (2012), p. 243

207 *ibid*, p. 243

the State, with an ideology based on myth; virile and anti-hedonistic, it is sacralised in a political religion affirming the absolute primacy of the nation understood as an ethnically homogeneous organic community, hierarchically organised into a corporative State, with a bellicose mission to achieve grandeur, power and conquest with the ultimate aim of creating a new order and a new civilisation.[208]

Gentile elaborates on this theme by suggesting that totalitarianism, as associated with fascism, is an experiment in political domination which is undertaken by revolutionary movement with what he describes as an 'integralist' concept of politics. He opines that it aspires to monopolise power, and whether power is secured by legal or illegal means, it destroys or transforms the previous regime.[209] Furthermore, totalitarianism involves constructing a new state based on a regime of single party government, with the main objective being to conquer the society through the subordination, integration and homogenisation of those that are governed, based on the integral politicisation of existence.[210] Gentile suggests that this occurs whether it is collective or individual, and: 'interpreted according to the categories, myths and values of a palingenetic ideology.'[211] It is suggested that these values are institutionalised in the

---

208 Emilio Gentile, Fascism, Totalitarianism and Political Religion: Definitions and Critical Reflections on Criticism of an Interpretation, *Totalitarian Movements and Political Religions*, 5 (3) (Winter 2004), p. 329
209 *Ibid*, pp. 327–328
210 *Ibid*, pp. 327–328
211 *Ibid*, pp. 327–328

form of a political religion, which aims to shape the individual and the masses through what Gentile describes as an 'anthropological revolution' which aspires to regenerate human beings and create new men who are fully dedicated to realising the revolutionary and idealist policies of the party in power, with the ultimate goal of creating new civilisations beyond the Nation State.[212]

Debate over what attracts people to fascism has been concerned primarily with issues of demagoguery, opportunism and terror.[213] Primo Levi felt that this helped to disguise the appeal of fascism, when he noted that people knew of or remembered that when Hitler and Mussolini gave public speeches they were not just believed, they were also applauded, admired and adored as if they were gods.[214] It is suggested–and this may be a factor in contemporary populist nationalist politicians–that they were charismatic leaders: 'who possessed the secret power to seduce which did not derive from any real credibility or from the justness of the things they said, but from the 'fascinating' way in which those things were said, from their eloquence, their histrionic art, maybe instinctive or maybe patiently exercised and learned.'[215]

In considering contemporary populist leaders it is worth noting Gentile's observations about totalitarian and fascist leaders, that the ideas they proposed were not the same all of the time, and that even though they were generally 'aberrant, foolish, or cruel,' they were still cheered and followed

---

212 *ibid*, pp. 327–328
213 *ibid*, pp. 332–333
214 *ibid*, pp. 332–333
215 *ibid*, pp. 332–333

by millions.[216] The candidacy and Presidency of Donald Trump has been marked by policies targeting Mexicans, Hispanics, transgender military personnel, and Muslims. Such policies contradict much that is deemed to be acceptable in U.S politics but they have received popular support. There has been continued support despite the mockery of disabled reporters, a blanket denouncement of elements of the press as fake, threats to protesters, misogyny, and apparently narcissistic and egocentric claims of self-importance, crowd sizes, or personal popularity.

Tony Michels observes that on the road to the White House, Trump understood that words and actions previously deemed unacceptable actually served him well. As he states: 'The more lies he told, the more boorishly he behaved, the more bigotry he espoused, the more ignorance he revealed, the more defiance he displayed, all the more approval he gained.'[217] Michels elaborates that: 'Trump's victory signals a rupture in American political traditions' and that Republican control of Congress and the White House allows Trump to pursue his election promise to 'make America great again.'[218] It is proposed by Michels that a rightward trajectory has been seen in American politics since 1968 and the presidential bid of George Wallace. Although Wallace lost to Nixon he had shown the possibility of luring white workers away from the Democratic Party through racial appeals. The Republicans noticed this.[219]

---

216 *ibid*, pp. 332–333
217 Tony Michels, Donald Trump and the Triumph of Anti-liberalism, *Jewish Social Studies: History, Culture, Society*, 22 (3) (Spring Summer 2017), p. 186
218 *ibid*, p. 186
219 *ibid*, p. 187

Michels suggests that the rise of the Christian right in the late 1970s is another factor, with evangelicals organising campaigns against legalised abortion, equal rights for women, gay rights, and the separation of the church and the state in public schools. Such groups established themselves in the Republican Party.[220] Conservative Christianity is also seen as a factor in groups such as Britain First which will be detailed later.

Another factor in the increased relevance and influence or right wing politics in the U.S was economics and the role of the state. In 1980 President Reagan, in response to the recession stated that: 'Government is not the solution to our problems. Government is the problem.'[221] Reagan called for deregulation, privatisation, lower taxes, austerity, and uncontrolled trade. Other Republicans supported the ideas of Reagan and gained a coalition of working-class whites, middle-classes from the suburbs, white southerners, social conservative Protestants and Catholics, and the leaders of corporate business.[222]

An added phase in the movement of the Republican Party to the far-right is the Tea Party. For the Tea Party federal intervention in the economy was seen as a problem, and there was a demand for greater tax cuts and the break-up of government agencies. The Tea Party has shown a propensity to disrupt Washington and has refused to offer constructive alternatives.[223] The Tea Party was particularly hostile to the government of President Obama and rebelled against the Republican Party when it was felt it was not being obstruc-

---

220 *ibid*, p. 187
221 *ibid*, pp. 187–188
222 *ibid*, pp. 187–188
223 *ibid*, p. 189

tive enough. Michels suggests that Trump rose to power on the back of momentum created by the Tea Party-an outgrowth of Reagan's revolution, which was: 'a reaction to desegregation, the social movements of the 1960s, and the recession of the 1970s.'[224] Observers note that one of the surprises about Trump's election victory is that he is obviously unfit for that office based on standards that had previously been accepted. He has no political experience, clear leanings towards authoritarianism, and demonstrates repeated dishonesty.[225]

Alarmingly, in a book discussing the risks of tribalism, Trump has demonstrated and stirred up hostility towards Mexicans, Muslims and African Americans. It is asserted by Michels that he has also contributed to a rise in anti-Semitism with images of money and the Star of David being used in his election campaign to warn against the powerful forces in Washington.[226] Trump has exploited the populist potential of social media. He has Tweeted postings by white supremacist groups, and one of his closest advisors is head of a far-right online publication that has included headlines referring to a 'Republican Spoiler' as a 'Renegade Jew.'[227] Trump also repeatedly refers to 'America First' despite being advised of its pro-Nazi associations in the 1930s, and has been reluctant to condemn white supremacists.[228] Previous Republican governments have been accused of neo-conservatism and a desire to spread democracy and American influence worldwide. Trump campaigned on an

---

224 *ibid*, p. 189
225 *ibid*, p. 190
226 *ibid*, p. 190
227 *ibid*, p. 190
228 *ibid*, p. 190

agenda of isolationism.[229] Michels suggests that at worst Trump has given encouragement to anti-Semitism, and at best he has tolerated it.[230]

The appeal of political leaders such as Donald Trump is not always apparent to observers, but, as Gentile notes, and this needs to be considered with followers of many populist nationalist politicians: 'We should remember that those believers, including the diligent executors of inhuman orders, were not born torturers, nor monsters (save a few exceptions): they were ordinary people.'[231] Elaborating on this theme, Gentile notes that although monsters do exist, there are not as many as to be really dangerous. He suggests that the man in the street is much more dangerous, as is the servant who is ready to believe and obey without ordering.[232] He suggests that such servants include those: 'Like Eichmann, like Höss, the commander of Auschwitz, like Stangl, the commander of Treblinka, like the French soldiers twenty years later, the slaughterers in Algeria, like the American soldiers thirty years later, the slaughterers in Vietnam'.[233] Gentile is of course describing the very ordinariness of many who commit acts of barbarity and cruelty towards others. It is not implied that all populist politicians, or those that support them, are capable of inspiring or participating in acts of cruelty, but Gentile's observations are worthy of note and contemplation.

---

229 *ibid*, p. 189

230 *ibid*, p. 190

231 Emilio Gentile, Fascism, Totalitarianism and Political Religion, pp. 332–333

232 *ibid*, pp. 332–333

233 *ibid*, pp. 332–333

The populist and far-right political parties of Europe are varied. Alternative fur Deutschland (AfD) in Germany has managed to gain representation in ten of the sixteen state parliaments since September 2016. AfD started off as a party with a Eurosceptic focus but since 2016 it has been an anti-Islam party that also wants Germany to stop atoning for Nazi crimes.[234] The Hungarian Jobbik party or Movement for a Better Hungary has been the country's third largest party since 2014. It has a reputation for anti-Semitism and a preoccupation with Hungarian ethnicity and hostility towards Israel.[235] The Front National in France is marked by its strong anti-immigrant rhetoric.[236] In Greece, Golden Dawn are seen as neo-fascists with an expressed admiration for Hitler. The leader of Golden Dawn has claimed that the gas chambers are a lie. The party exploits problems linked to the refugee crisis from the war in Syria. Golden dawn claims to a Greek nationalist movement rather than neo-Nazi.[237] Freiheitliche Partei Österreichs (FPÖ) in Austria is accused of having Nazi sympathies and is vocally anti-Islam.[238] The Sweden Democrats are also anti-immigrant and the leadership express admiration for President Trump.[239] The Danish People's Party, in a similarity to President Trump, calls for cuts to immigration from Muslim countries.[240]

---

234 Anoosh Chakelian, Rise of The Nationalists: Europe's Far-Right Parties, *New Statesman*, (3–9 March 2017), p. 30

235 *ibid*, p. 30

236 *ibid*, p. 30

237 *ibid*, p. 30

238 *ibid*, p. 30

239 *ibid*, p. 30

240 *ibid*, p. 30

Geert Wilders of the Dutch Partij voor de Vrijheid has been described as the man who invented Trumpism.[241]

The elections to the European Parliament in 2014 were characterised by the success of far-right Eurosceptic parties.[242] It is suggested that the inability of mainstream parties to deal with domestic issues opened up a space for far-right parties to capitalise on.[243] Most notably these parties and groups made scapegoats of the European Union (EU) by using domestic welfare issues and making them EU issues through anti-immigration discourse and emphasis on national sovereignty.[244] Daphne Halikiopoulou and Sofia Vasilopoulou suggest that these parties: 'adopt a narrative that links the salient issue of the economy with questions such as immigration, citizenship law, employment law and the EU more broadly.'[245]

The far-right and Eurosceptic groups blame the EU for problems with unemployment, economic hardship, and general discontent, due to policies of freedom of movement and relaxed immigration controls. This, in turn, increases competition for resources that are considered to be scarce due to the state of economies in the EU region.[246] This results in a sense of competition between those who perceive themselves as the rightful beneficiaries of welfare, and foreigners, with the added concept that foreigners are alien

---

241 *ibid,* p. 30

242 Daphne Halikiopoulou and Sofia Vasilopoulou, Support for the Far Right in the 2014 European Parliament Elections: A Comparative Perspective, *The Political Quarterly,* 85 (3) (July-September 2014), p. 285

243 *ibid,* p. 285

244 *ibid,* p. 285

245 *ibid,* p. 285

246 *ibid,* p. 285

to the belief system, ideas, values and principles of each nation.[247] From this Halikiopoulou and Vasilopoulou conclude that for the far-right:

> …the EU is presented as an institution that violates the principles of the social contract upon which the nation is premised. Through this narrative, far-right parties have succeeded in redefining the debate on Europe and immigration. Their success has triggered a response from some mainstream parties who are echoing the far-right in their adoption of stricter immigration policies and calls to revert more power back to the nation-state.[248]

The far-right label is broad. As Halikiopoulou and Vasilopoulou note, those far-right parties that have gained electoral success in the European Parliament range: 'from the populist right in the UK, through the populist radical right in Denmark, Sweden and the Netherlands and a revamped extreme right-wing party with strong past fascist associations in France, to the openly extreme right in Greece and Hungary.'[249]

Halikiopoulou and Vasilopoulou suggest that the far-right can be distinguished from other political groupings by three characteristics: nativism (nationalism), authoritarianism, and populism. However they also clarify that the extent to which this characteristics are exhibited varies in degree and type, and that the crucial factor is the relationship with democracy and violence, and the stance with

---

247 *ibid*, p. 285
248 *ibid*, p. 285
249 *ibid*, p. 287

the wider system.[250] It is further suggested that whilst the Greek Golden Dawn (GD) and the British UKIP are both Euro-sceptic and concerned about ideas of sovereignty and nationhood, they also differ. GD is an extreme neo-Nazi party that wants to make all immigration illegal and defines nationality in terms of blood, birth and creed. UKIP generally emphasises civic values, economic issues, and considers the incompatibility of some belief systems.[251] However, as has been noted earlier, the UKIP manifesto in 2017 had multiple references to Islam and the Muslim community with regards to planned legislation.

The broader trend in Western Europe is that those parties experiencing an increase in support tend to emphasise ideology and values rather than ethnicity and blood. Such parties perceive immigration negatively not so much because immigrants are racially or ethnically different or inferior, but because they claim that the values of outsider groups threaten liberal democratic institutions.[252] In echoes of the 'in-group' and 'out-group' conflicts discussed earlier, the outsiders are portrayed as being hostile to societal norms and unwilling to obey laws. The emphasis of some political groups is on the idea of maintaining Western values.[253]

It is apparent that unfavourable attitudes towards immigrants are the most important predictors in explaining the support for right wing political parties.[254] Schmuck and

---

250 *ibid*, p. 287
251 *ibid*, pp. 287–288
252 *ibid*, pp. 287–288
253 *ibid*, pp. 287
254 Desirée Schmuck and Jörg Matthes, How Anti-immigrant Right-wing Populist Advertisements Affect Young Voters:

Matthes note that a wealth of theories suggest that ethnic threats lead groups to prejudice, as seen in realistic group theory, conflict theory, symbolic racism, and social dominance theory.[255] The integrated threat theory of prejudice suggests that realistic economic threats, as well as symbolic threats posed by immigrants, may lead to ethnic prejudice.[256] Right wing political groups make use of perceived economic and symbolic threats posed by immigrants and use them in advertisements.[257] By applying cultural threats such groups seek to imply that the 'in-group's' values system is being undermined by an 'out-group', and this is achieved by political posters using distorted pictures of specific social groups and religions, especially Islam.[258]

The tribalism of such campaigns and the implied danger from an 'out-group' is used by most far-right political groups. The 'out-group' targets are invariably immigrants (economic or refugee) and minority faiths, in particular Islam. Social media has enhanced the potential for far-right groups to spread their message. Notable of such groups is Britain First in the UK along with allied campaign movements such as the English Defence League (EDL).[259] Britain First combined the strategies of the EDL–street protest and

---

Symbolic Threats, Economic Threats and the Moderating Role of Education, *Journal of Ethnic and Migration Studies*, 41 (10) (2015), p. 1580

255 *ibid*, p. 1580

256 *ibid*, p. 1580

257 *ibid*, pp. 1580–1581

258 *ibid*, pp. 1580–1581

259 Chris Allen, Britain First: The 'Frontline Resistance' to the Islamification of Britain, *The Political Quarterly*, 85 (3) (July-September 2014), p. 354

social media–with the strategies of the British National Party (BNP)–political campaigning in elections.[260]

The origins of Britain First may hint at some religious fundamentalism and zealotry. It was created by former BNP member James Dowson, a Scottish Calvinist minister with a close relationship to loyalist paramilitaries in Northern Ireland. Dowson has been described as an evangelical Protestant.[261] Dowson left the BNP after the general election campaign in 2010, following which he linked up with former BNP councillor Paul Golding to create and launch Britain First in May 2011.[262]

The group claimed an aim to protect British and Christian morality.[263] Using their BNP contacts they approached around 40,000 potential supporters.[264] Chris Allen suggests that 'far-right' is a convenient umbrella term when in reality those who support Britain First are more disparate, diverse, and divergent. However he observes that some common themes of ideology are apparent including populist nationalism, and an aim to maintain and strengthen the British Union and its sovereignty whilst celebrating the identities and cultures of England, Scotland, Wales, and Northern Ireland.[265] Britain First is resistant to interference from the EU, and seeks to preserve what they perceive to be Britain's ethnic and cultural heritage, traditions, customs and values.[266]

---

260 *ibid*, p. 354

261 *ibid*, p. 355

262 *ibid*, p. 355

263 *ibid*, p. 355

264 *ibid*, p. 355

265 *ibid*, p. 355

266 *ibid*, p. 355

As Allen observes, as is traditional with the far-right, nationalism and ideas of race, blood, and nativism are directly linked.[267] There is a call for an immediate halt to immigration to preserve the existence of indigenous British people, and, in a similarity to far-right groups in other countries, Christianity is also integral as it is seen to be the foundation of British society and culture.[268] The anti-fascist group Hope Not Hate (a U.K based advocacy group) claim that: 'within Britain First's hierarchy something of a dooms-day prophecy exists, where the end of civilisation follows an apocalyptic battle between Christians and Muslims.'[269] Britain First adopts more aggressive tactics towards Muslim communities. Most notably, apart from frequent street protests, there have been staged and filmed 'invasions' of mosques. Members of the group enter these places of worship and confront worshippers with arguments about Britain being a Christian country, the failure of the Muslim community to stop grooming gangs, the need to read the Bible, and asserting that Mohammad is a false prophet. They have also aggressively forced Muslims to accept copies of British army Bibles.[270]

In a development that fits in with some definitions of fascism as detailed earlier, there is an increasingly militaristic element to Britain First. There are allegations that it has created combat training for members, that it is prepared to fight for its cause, reference to battalions, and even the use of former army vehicles during its 'Christian Patrols' in predominantly Muslim areas. As Allen observes, this carries

---

267 *ibid,* p. 355
268 *ibid,* pp. 356–357
269 *ibid,* p. 357
270 *ibid,* p. 358

with it an insidious and dangerous message.[271] The message from Britain First is that all Muslims are the same (this will include Muslim refugees from war-torn lands) and that they should be seen equally as a threat to British and Western society. There is a large emphasis on Christianity and the concept of an apocalyptic conflict with Islam.[272] Allen asserts that Britain First, and by implication other similar groups, are potentially dangerous.[273]

Propaganda in its varied forms is a factor in the appeal of populist nationalist and far-right political groups. Some people may be more susceptible to the persuasive powers of propaganda. Most research on ethnic attitudes reveals a strong negative correlation between formal education and prejudice against ethnic minorities.[274] As Schmuck and Matthes observe, in reviewing multiple studies: 'formal education level was the most important socio-structural characteristic in perceiving a threat from immigrants and ethnic minorities.'[275] An assumption is made that formal education may moderate the effect of populist advertisements (and this book asserts, by implication, propaganda and peer influence) on people's overall attitudes.[276] Research also suggests that individual variables such as intelligence, political knowledge, political awareness, issue-specific knowledge, or formal education can moderate communication effects.[277] Studies show that individuals who are more intelligent as

---

271 *ibid*, p. 360

272 *ibid*, p. 360

273 *ibid*, p. 360

274 Desirée Schmuck and Jörg Matthes, Right Wing Populist Advertisements, p. 1583

275 *ibid*, p. 1583

276 *ibid*, p. 1583

277 *ibid*, p. 1583

well as more politically attentive are more likely to receive a message, but less likely to be influenced by its persuasive content.[278] Furthermore it is shown that knowledgeable citizens are less likely to change their opinions when faced with new but irrelevant or misleading information, but if the new information is relevant or compelling, the better informed individuals tend to change their opinions more than those who are less informed.[279] Additionally, studies show that those with higher levels of attitude-relevant information tend to base their changes of opinion on the quality of the message content, while individuals with lower levels rely on superficial cues such as the length of the message.[280] The impact of media–which will include political broadcasts and news reports-is varied, with more knowledgeable individuals being more resistant to the influence of positive or negative news portrayals of immigrants; but Schmuck and Matthes accept that scholars have operationalised knowledge in different ways.[281]

Mary E. Wheeler and Susan T. Fiske cite multiple research studies to observe that the amygdala is involved in: 'sensing, relaying, and learning about potential danger represented by stimuli, whether via previous direct experience with an aversive stimulus, as in fear conditioning, or via indirect experience through social signals communicated by fear or anger in other individuals' facial expressions.'[282]

---

278 *ibid*, p. 1583

279 *ibid*, pp. 1583–1584

280 *ibid*, pp. 1583–1584

281 *ibid*, pp. 1583–1584

282 Mary E. Wheeler and Susan T. Fiske, Controlling Racial Prejudice: Social-Cognitive Goals Affect Amygdala and Stereotype Activation, *Psychological Science,* 16 (1) (2005), p. 56

As their study notes, the amygdala responds to anticipated or imagined aversive events that can be learned even through verbal communication.[283] This clearly implies that some prejudice responses may be due to learned fear. Conversely the results of Wheeler and Fiske's research show that perceivers can change the social context in which they view an individual and this can affect 'out-group' perception as measured in brain and reaction time behaviour.[284] Elaborating on this theme they observe that the default differential response can evaporate, with a conscious effort to individuate. It was noted that regardless of an individual's long-term tendencies toward prejudice, responses to targets of prejudice varied with controllable processing goals.[285] The experiments that Wheeler and Fiske referred to were focused on racial stereotyping by White American participants, but it is stated that other research shows that both Blacks and Whites tend to categorise their respective 'out-group' and that prejudices extend to other categories including other ethnic, gender, and age groups.[286]

Amygdala activity suggests a biological response to a real or imagined threat, somewhat akin to fight or flight. This does not excuse the response or the prejudice but it medicalises the biological reactions that occur. Schmuck and Matthes observed that threat appeals do not affect all young adults in the same way. Economic threat appeals are noted to increase negative attitudes towards immigrants in less educated young adults, but more highly educated young adults were resistant the effects of the same threat.

---

283 *ibid,* p. 56
284 *ibid,* p. 61
285 *ibid,* p. 61
286 *ibid,* p. 61

The suggestion is that economic threat appeals are more powerful among less educated younger voters.[287]

A rationale offered for this is due to the career situation of young adults with lower formal education as they may already be in employment, and as such job security will be more of an issue than with young adults in high school or those attending or going to attend university.[288] Those who leave education early face more difficulties in the labour market than those who continue with their studies, and as immigrants in European societies on average have a lower level of formal education than the average majority population of young adults there will be direct competition for jobs and housing.[289] Young majority population citizens may feel that their status and resources are under threat, and as such the economic threat will be perceived as very real.[290]

Schmuck and Matthes also observed that the impact of symbolic threat appeals in right wing populist advertising did not depend on formal education levels in young voters, and exposure to symbolic threat advertisements led to a significant increase in negative attitudes towards immigrants among all young voters.[291] It is suggested that perceived threats to cultural identity are more general than economic threats, but perceived economic threats impact more greatly on those who lack a formal education.[292] For those without formal education there is fear of loss of employment or

---

287 Desirée Schmuck and Jörg Matthes, Right Wing Populist Advertisements, pp. 1590–1591
288 *ibid*, pp. 1590–1591
289 *ibid*, pp. 1590–1591
290 *ibid*, pp. 1590–1591
291 *ibid*, pp. 1590–1591
292 *ibid*, pp. 1590–1591

housing opportunities, but for those with or without formal education the feared loss of cultural or national identity is a shared concern. Symbolic threat appeals in political advertising induce negative attitudes towards immigration among young adults.[293] Political voting does not dictate the impact of political advertising. Schmuck and Matthes note that:

> ...it is important to note that the effects of political advertisements did not depend on young voters' political ideology. This result is striking because it signals that political predispositions did not protect young voters against the influence of right-wing populist campaigns. In other words, even if young voters lean to the left, right-wing populist ads can be successful in activating symbolic and—depending on education—economic threats. This finding underlines the ultimate strength of populist appeals.[294]

This is an important observation. The appeal of far-right advertising, and therefore propaganda and rhetoric, can cross the political spectrum. As such traditional left of centre voters will support far-right candidates and political groups based on the simplicity and apparent plausibility of the message being delivered.

Populist and far-right politicians (and some mainstream politicians) tap into this fear of symbolic and economic threat. In the UK they are assisted with elements of the popular printed press which are avowedly hostile towards

---

293 *ibid*, pp. 1590–1591
294 *ibid*, pp. 1590–1591

the EU and are anti-migrant. Whether or not these newspapers are purchased, the headlines demonising the EU, and also migrants and refugees, will be seen in multiple retail outlets. This must have an impact. In the U.S the election campaign and subsequent Presidency of Donald Trump was markedly hostile to others–Muslims, migrants, Mexicans, and Hispanics–and played on the ideas of economic and symbolic threat. By tapping into populist ideas of isolationism with 'America First' and nationalism with 'Make America Great Again' Trump was able to use the fears of the poorly educated who were concerned about job losses, and the more general population's fear of losing cultural identity and dangers from terrorism and crime. The same tactics are used by far-right and populist nationalist politicians in Europe, the UK, and Australasia.

Propaganda is a factor in polarising populations and the dehumanisation of 'out-groups.' Propaganda does not have to be wholly truthful, it has to convey a message which is acceptable to the recipient. Far-right groups thrive on persuading the 'in-group' that the 'out-group' is a danger. This may be through exaggerated claims of threat or by using plausible evidence through the selective use of information. As Joseph Goebbels wrote in 1927: 'Christ did not offer proofs in his Sermon on the Mount. He simply made assertions. Self-evident truths don't have to be proven.'[295] Hitler also observed that: 'Propaganda works on the general public from the standpoint of an idea and makes them ripe for the victory of this idea, while the organization achieves victory by the persistent, organic, and militant union of those supporters who seem willing and able to carry on the fight

---

295 Peter Longerich, Goebbels, (London: 2015), p. 79

for victory.[296] He added that: 'The first task of propaganda is to win people for subsequent organization; the first task of organization is to win men for the continuation of propaganda. The second task of propaganda is the disruption of the existing state of affairs and the permeation of this state of affairs with the new doctrine, while the second task of organization must be the struggle for power, thus to achieve the final success of the doctrine.'[297]

Many far-right and populist nationalist groups use sweeping generalisations to allude to a potential threat to the 'in-group' from various 'out-groups.' Facts are not necessarily provided insofar as a whole religious community can be demonised and dehumanised as terrorists or sex offenders; refugees are portrayed as a threat-particularly if they are male; migrants are responsible for job losses, taking housing, and draining valuable resources. Evidence is not required for this in the same way that Goebbels did not need to provide proof. When it is suggested that entire populations of other nations will potentially move to another recipient country, those who are susceptible to such propaganda do not question the obvious mendacity of the claim or the clear unlikelihood that it is true. Similarly, attacks on minority religions–increasingly Islam–will selectively cherry-pick verses from the Qur'an to show that Muslims are a threat. No reference is made to violent texts from the Old Testament, even though it is a scripture shared by Christians, Jews, and Muslims.

Some vocal far-right activists will, with apparent credibility, cite the Qur'an in a manner that they perceive provides indisputable proof of their arguments against

---

296 Adolf Hitler, Mein Kampf, p. 530
297 *ibid,* p. 530

Islam. This is certainly a tactic employed by Britain First and the English Defence League in the U.K. The similarity of this approach to that of the Nazis can be observed from the work of Dr Douglas M. Kelley, one of the psychiatrists tasked with assessing the Nazi defendants at the International Military Tribunal in Nuremberg. In his book summarising the assessments he discussed Julius Streicher, editor of *Der Stürmer,* a notorious anti-Semitic Nazi publication. Kelley observed that the only books that Streicher was interested in were those that: 'dealt with the Jewish problem, or which gave him material for discussion in the light of his own familiarity with the subject.'[298] Kelley noted that for months before Streicher stood trial, and even during the trial period, he was engaged in a detailed analysis of the Bible as he was: 'determined to demonstrate that, even in their own writings, the Jewish people have condemned themselves.'[299]

Are far-right groups in Britain, continental Europe, North America, and Australasia fascist or akin to Nazis? Some groups proudly assume a Nazi or neo-Nazi label. Others, most notably the populist nationalist groups deny such an accusation.

As James Q. Whitman observes, the second volume of Mein Kampf in 1927, made clear Hitler's vision for the revival of Germany. His vision drew on the Nazi Party Programme of 1920 in which five of twenty-five points involved citizenship, which was to be restricted to people of German blood, plus a policy on disabilities of foreign residents who were to

---

298 Dr Douglas M. Kelley, 22 Cells in Nuremberg, (London: 1947), p. 118
299 *Ibid,* p. 119

be threatened with expulsion.[300] The five points referred to
have an uncanny similarity to policies associated with contemporary populist nationalist groups, and with avowedly
far-right groups:

4. Only a *Volk-* comrade *[Volksgenosse]* can be a citizen *[Staatsburger]*. Only a person or German blood,
   without regard to religion, can be a *Volk*-comrade.
   Accordingly no Jew can be a *Volk*-comrade.
5. Any person who is not a citizen should be able to live
   in German merely as a guest, and must be subject to
   legislation for foreigners.
6. Only a citizen is permitted the right to decide on the
   leadership [führung] and laws of the state. Therefore
   we demand that every public office, regardless of
   what kind, regardless of whether it is an office of
   the Reich, or any municipality, be accessible only to
   citizens...
7. We demand that the state obligate itself to provide
   the opportunities and wherewithal of life in the first
   instance strictly for citizens. If it is not possible to
   provide sustenance for the entire population, then
   nationals of foreign countries (non-citizens) must be
   expelled from the Reich.
8. All further immigration of non-Germans is to be
   prevented. We demand that all non-Germans who
   have immigrated into Germany since 2 August 1914,
   be immediately compelled to leave the Reich.[301]

---

300 James Q. Whitman, Hitler's American Model: The United
    States and the Making of Nazi Race Law, (Princeton: 2017),
    pp. 44–45
301 *ibid,* pp. 44–45

As Whitman properly observes: 'These demands, which anticipate so much of the far-right agitation that is troubling Europe again today, established the propositions that would be fundamental to Nazi citizenship law as it emerged at Nuremberg in 1935.'[302] One merely has to add to the Nazi references to immigrants and to Jews (in accepting the ongoing contemporary problems with anti-Semitism), the further targets of Muslims, refugees, ethnic and racial minorities, or those with a cultural or language heritage that differs from the majority more powerful or 'in-group' to see parallels that are glaringly obvious.

This book will not be discussing Islamist groups such as Daesh (Islamic State). However, their centralised military and paramilitary methods, combined with subjugation, mass murder, enslavement, contempt for any outside of the group, and aims at dominance of geographical areas and populations have, it is asserted, many factors that would potentially define them as fascist. Those factors are combined with distorted religious fundamentalism and a literalist, inflexible interpretation of the Qur'an. Daesh and other similar groups also show utter contempt for human life, and terrorist acts committed by them, and inspired by them, cause immense harm to innocents.

---

302 *ibid,* pp. 44–45

Conclusion

It is asserted that many far-right and populist national-ist groups pose a risk to the security and stability of host nations, specifically to those minority groups identified as 'out-groups' due to their ethnicity, racial heritage, culture, linguistic background, or faith. Some far-right groups freely accept being referred to as neo-Nazi or supremacist, in ways that affiliate them closely with the politics, policies, and ideas of National Socialism and other fascist regimes. Some groups, particularly those referred to herein as populist nationalist, may reject such comparisons, but elements of the policies they propose, the rhetoric used, and the casual demonising and dehumanising of 'out-group' others, would translate and transfer easily into the policies of fascists and neo-Nazis.

Many of the studies referred to within this book have considered the idea of the 'in-group' and 'out-group,' particularly with regard to prejudice by the former towards the latter. The ultimate example of such hostility was the regime of National Socialist Germany which led to the murder of millions of innocent civilians due to the 'out-group' status they were labelled with based on religion, ethnicity, nationality, culture, age, disability, gender, and politics. The most notable victims of Nazi crimes were Jews, Slavs and Roma. In the civil war in former Yugoslavia, Bosnian Serb forces committed genocide at Srebrenica with the methodical murder of over 7,000 Muslim men and boys. Further acts of mass murder occurred during that war in which civilians were specifically targeted because of their faith and cultural difference, even though they were part of established communities.

Reference has been made herein to the concept of economic threat and symbolic threat. It is asserted that when both threats are perceived by the majority or more powerful 'in-group' the risks of violence, crime, and genocide towards the minority and potentially weaker 'out-group' increases.

Jews in Nazi Germany were perceived as both an economic and a symbolic or cultural threat. They were held to be responsible for Germany's defeat in the First World War, for the subsequent social upheaval, for the financial difficulties that struck down the economy, and for the threat of Bolshevism. Concrete evidence was not needed to justify claims against the Jews, and Nazi propaganda fell on receptive ears. A gradual process denied Jews normal citizenship rights and sought, successfully, to dehumanise them in the eyes of the majority population. The war in Yugoslavia had multiple causes, not least of which was Serbian nationalism and expansionism, but in the process of expansionism, and resistance to territorial aims at independence, there was targeting and murder of those perceived as an economic (territorial) and symbolic threat.

Far-right groups such as Golden Dawn and Jobbik are comfortably described as having fascist or neo-Nazi leanings, particularly with their idea of ethnic purity in Greece and Hungary, and their hostility towards migrant or minority communities. Britain First, and with it the English Defence League (EDL), are nationalistic in outlook. They perceive a threat from the EU and those whose heritage is not obviously Anglo-Saxon, Celtic or Northern European. They are hostile towards migrants based upon ethnicity or religion. There is particular hostility towards Muslims, whether they are fully domiciled citizens, economic migrants, refugees, devoutly religious, or Muslim in heritage only. For Britain First there is the added element of a perceived war against Islam, which in part is based upon Christian fundamentalist ideas. The more extreme far-right groups share a sense of absolutism in their belief in the certainty of their cause, and literalism in how they interpret the threats and dangers they perceive. The absolutists and literalists of the extreme far-right are not open to debate. In this they share a commonality with the religious fundamentalists that lean towards acts of terrorism who are equally unwilling to consider an alternative opinion.

The United Kingdom Independence Party (UKIP) originated as a political party seeking to secure Britain's exit from the EU. UKIP is generally perceived as a populist nationalist group. They seek to return Britain to an ideal of past independence without the influence of the EU. But campaigning in the 2016 referendum about whether Britain should remain in or leave the EU was markedly anti-migrant and caused uproar when a poster was used depicting a line of refugees entering another country with the tag-line 'Breaking Point.' The implication was clear that those refugees were heading towards Britain and that Britain was unable to cope with them. There was no hint at compassion for their plight or personal circumstances, nor was there clarification to specify that the actual destination of the refugees was not to Britain. During the 2017 General Election the UKIP manifesto referred to forced physical examination of female children under the age of 16 based upon their heritage (non-European) with a supposed aim to protect their welfare from Female Genital Mutilation. There were proposals to ban the burqa and niqab, with many disingenuous rationales offered to justify this. The manifesto sought, or at least managed, to isolate and categorise Muslims as 'others' or part of the 'out-group.' Britain First, the EDL, and UKIP clearly seek to categorise migrants and Muslims as economic and symbolic threats.

The election campaign and subsequent Presidency of Donald Trump has used economic and symbolic threats (including security threats) against Muslims, Hispanics, Mexicans and migrants. Trump has referred to 'America First' (isolationism and protectionism) and 'Make America Great Again' (nationalism).

Furthermore, the use of economic and symbolic threats by far-right and populist nationalist groups implies, with or without evidence, that the 'out-groups' will take jobs, housing, opportunities, and prosperity. It is further implied that they will also contribute to an eradication of culture, and national identity, as well as presenting a risk of crime and dangers to national security. Implication without solid evidence is not proof, but as Goebbels stated, self-evident truths do not have to be proven.[303]

It has been noted that the far-right can be distinguished from other political groupings by three key characteristics: nativism (nationalism), authoritarianism, and populism; all factors that are apparent in the policies and rhetoric of the far-right and populist nationalist groups mentioned herein.[304]

---

303 Peter Longerich, Goebbels, p. 79
304 Daphne Halikiopoulou and Sofia Vasilopoulou, Support for the Far Right, p. 287

Returning to Gregory H. Stanton's Ten Stages of Genocide: Classification, Symbolisation, Discrimination, Dehumanisation, Organisation, Polarisation, Preparation, Persecution, Extermination and Denial.[305] This book asserts that some of these stages have been reached in many westernised democracies–most notably Classification, Discrimination, Dehumanisation, and Polarisation. To some extent Symbolisation has been reached in that some communities are defined by attire that denotes their difference, and are demonised and dehumanised by virtue of perceived differences that can be readily identified by the 'in-group.' This does not of course imply that there is a risk of genocide in Europe, Australasia, or the United States, but it is asserted that the elements for serious harm are in place.

Forced assimilation of minority communities is not the answer. That would reinforce the idea that those communities are 'the other' and part of an 'out-group.' Shared language and common values will help promote tolerance and integration, but banning cultural attire, religions, first or family languages, and heritage symbols, helps to ostracise and demonise minorities as not belonging to the main population or community. The research referred to earlier suggests that education is required. Minority communities need to be accepted as part of a wider whole society, including those differences that may be attributed to ethnic background, culture, and religion. The threat perceived by majority communities can be reduced by simply raising awareness and understanding of those who live among them, study with them, work with them, and share similar aspirations.

---

305 Gregory H. Stanton, Genocide Watch

Research cited shows that poorly educated young people (and it is assumed older people) are more likely to perceive an economic threat from immigrants than those with a higher education and political knowledge. Poorly educated people are receptive to brief propaganda and are less likely to be persuaded to change opinion. Both poorly educated and better educated people are receptive to propaganda suggesting that immigrants pose a symbolic threat that may impact upon culture and national identity. Merely dismissing fears of economic and symbolic threat as being evidence of racism or intolerance is not constructive. Those fears have to be recognised and understood, and then reduced by use of evidence rather than simplistic rhetoric. Improved education, including political and cultural awareness may reduce the susceptibility to propaganda messages. Without forcing assimilation, it would be logical to encourage children of mixed backgrounds and heritage into shared educational settings with the majority population to lessen the perception of difference and otherness at an early age. Where education occurs separately due to faith or gender specific schooling, opportunities should be provided for activities with other communities.

Mainstream politicians need to consider the rhetoric that they use, and the potential that words have to cause harm. The popular media too, must consider how headlines and articles may promote hate, intolerance, prejudice and fear. The nature and tone of news broadcasts and articles can emphasise difference rather than commonality. The information that populations receive from trusted sources—politicians and the media—has an influence on attitudes and the consequences of those attitudes. Restraint and the exercising of social responsibility does not take away the right to campaign, to raise concerns about socially pertinent issues, or to report the news, or to promote an opinion. Learning the lessons of history must include recognising the potential for harm that words, action, inaction, and complicity can cause. The research leads to the following assertions:

- Politicians at local, regional, national, and international level need to carefully consider rhetoric used. Words aimed at showing resolve and strength, or to appease and agitate core support, can have ramifications. This particularly applies when minority communities are made to appear as an 'out-group' that may be perceived as an economic, symbolic, cultural, or security threat to the 'in-group' by use of sweeping generalisations.
- The fears and anxieties of those who show intolerance need to be understood and recognised. Failure to address such concerns will not alleviate them.
- Some political groups, politicians, elements of the press, and members of the public refer to asylum seekers, refugees, and those who travel from foreign lands without visas as 'illegals.' Similarly members of what may be seen as 'out-groups' will be discussed or referred to dismissively as 'them' or 'they' or by the use of generically hostile terms such as 'vermin' and 'cockroach.' The implication is clear that such people are seen as being outside of the rule of law and undeserving of the protections that other citizens accept as normal. They are dehumanised, and dehumanisation is one of the risk factors in harm, and ultimately in genocide.
- The popular press should also consider its social responsibility. Headlines and articles aimed at pleasing the core market may cause harm due to the trust

that many place in news media outlets. Elements of the press publish articles that provocatively refer to religious and racial minorities, or migrants and refugees, in terms that may be alarmist and possibly aimed at inciting or encouraging hostility, blame, and distrust. Regulatory bodies need to deal with potential incitement towards hatred and intolerance that may cause harm. Advertisers should also consider their responsibilities to brands, shareholders, and customers.

– A free press is essential to report crime and criminality, to inform, to identify wrongdoing, and to hold governments at all levels to account. Governments that deny the freedom and autonomy of the press must be challenged by politicians, journalists, and the electorate.

– Human rights legislation should be enshrined in law, ideally to an internationally agreed standard, and the law must be upheld. The judiciary must be independent of government control in order to freely interpret and enforce the law.

– Freedom of thought, freedom of expression, freedom of speech, and freedom of religion need to be protected locally, regionally, nationally and internationally, but with the proviso that such freedoms come with responsibilities to uphold the law, protect rights, and not to incite hatred or crime.

– Educators should seek to improve awareness of cultural and religious differences and shared values within communities. Improved political education may offer protection from the negative and harmful impact of propaganda.

- Cultural and diversity awareness events should be encouraged, but these must be well advertised and broadly inclusive, rather than being limited mainly to attract attendees who are already receptive.
- Anti-racism campaigns should be proactive as well as reactive. There is a tendency to respond to hate events after they occur (which of course needs to happen) rather than seeking to inform and prevent such events.
- Religious and cultural leaders of all faiths and backgrounds need to reinforce and emphasise teachings that encourage tolerance, compassion and understanding.
- Legal frameworks should be used to identify and address hate crime in all of its forms. Making intolerance and hostility to minorities socially unacceptable, and criminalising acts when appropriate, will help to remove the normality or acceptability of prejudice.
- The international community should act to identify regimes with the potential for genocide and take such courses of action as deemed appropriate to prevent harm and save lives.

Zillmer *et al* noted that their review of the Rorschach tests conducted with the Nuremberg trial defendants, and with rank-and-file Nazis and collaborators, did not conclude that there was a homogeneous Nazi personality type marked by substantial and inevitable psychopathology.[306] It is worth noting that Dr Douglas M. Kelley, writing in 1946, argued

---

306 Eric A. Zillmer *et al*, The Quest for the Nazi Personality, p. 178

that the individuals evaluated at Nuremberg were neither insane nor unique, but that they could be: 'duplicated in any country of the world today.'[307] Kelley further suggested that: 'We must also realise that such personalities exist in this country (the United States), and that there are undoubtedly some individuals who would willingly climb over the corpses of one half of the people in the United States if, by doing so, they could therefore be given control of the other half.'[308] Over seventy years after those words were written by a professional who had spent months examining senior Nazis, there is a clear warning that should be heeded by many nations.

The crimes of the Axis powers led directly to the Universal Declaration of Human Rights and the United Nations Convention on the Prevention and Punishment of the Crime of Genocide. National and international governments have obligations in law. Whilst hate, prejudice, and intolerance does not automatically lead to genocide, it can lead to harm. Harm covers a broad spectrum from emotional harm to physical harm, but including financial harm, lack of opportunity (employment, financial, housing, healthcare, education); the removal of accepted protections in law, all forms of abuse, and ultimately the loss of life. Hate, prejudice, and intolerance must be challenged robustly, swiftly and consistently at all levels of society and government to protect those who potentially could be targeted.

The Holocaust and other genocides followed identifiable patterns as highlighted in this brief work. The information and the knowledge is there, warnings can be seen, and national and international communities understand the risks. Doing nothing is not an option.

---

307 *ibid,* p. 178
308 *ibid,* p. 178

Bibliography:

1. Allen, Chris, Britain First: The 'Frontline Resistance' to the Islamification of Britain, *The Political Quarterly*, 85 (3) (July-September 2014)

2. Anon, UKIP Manifesto 2017, www.ukip.org/manifesto2017, (2017)

3. Arendt, Hannah, Eichmann in Jerusalem: A Report on the Banality of Evil, (New York, Penguin Classics, 1977)

4. Brewer, Marilynn B, The Psychology of Prejudice: Ingroup Love or Outgroup Hate, *Journal of Social Issues*, 55 (3) (1999)

5. Cesarani, David, Final Solution, The Fate of The Jews 1933–49, (London, Macmillan 2016)

6. Chakelian, Anoosh, Rise of The Nationalists: Europe's Far-Right Parties, *New Statesman*, (3–9 March 2017)

7. Conces, Rory J, A Sisyphean Tale: The Pathology of Ethnic Nationalism and the Pedagogy of Forging Humane Democracies in the Balkans, *Studies in East European Thought*, 57 (2005)

8. Confino, Alon, Reflections. A world Without Jews: Interpreting the Holocaust, *German History*, 27 (4) (2009)

9. Earl, Hilary, Prosecuting Genocide Before the Genocide Convention: Raphael Lemkin and the Nuremberg Trials, 1945–1949, *Journal of Genocide Research*, 15 (3) (2013)

10. Evans, Richard J, The Third Reich in History and Memory, (London, Abacus 2015)

11. Gentile, Emilio, Fascism, Totalitarianism and Political Religion: Definitions and Critical Reflections on Criticism of an Interpretation, *Totalitarian Movements and Political Religions*, 5 (3) (Winter 2004)

12. Halikiopoulou, Daphne and Vasilopoulou, Sofia, Support for the Far Right in the 2014 European Parliament Elections: A Comparative Perspective, *The Political Quarterly*, 85 (3) (July-September 2014)

13. Harris, Lasana T and Fiske, Susan T, Dehumanising the Lowest of the Low: Neuroimaging Responses to Extreme Out-Groups, *Psychological Science*, 17 (10) (2006)

14. Heffer, Greg, *Sunday Express*, http://www.express.co.uk/news/politics/719871/Brexit-Treasury-Brexit-warning-EU-single-market-eebillion-Patrick-Minford-fifth-column, (11 October 2016)

15. Hitler, Adolf, Mein Kampf, Translated by Ralph Manheim, (London, Pimlico 2014)

16. Hoare, Marko Attila, Genocide in the Former Yugoslavia Before and After Communism, *EUROPE-ASIA STUDIES*, 62 (7) (September 2010)

17. Hook, Derek, Pre Discursive Racism, *Journal of Community & Applied Social Psychology*, 16 (2006)

18. Kelley, Douglas M, 22 Cells in Nuremberg, (London, W.H. Allen 1947)

19. Legault, Lisa and Green-Demers, Isabelle, The Protective Role of Self-Determined Prejudice Regulation in The Relationship Between Ingroup Threat and Prejudice, *Motivation & Emotion*, 36 (2012)

20. Longerich, Peter, Goebbels, (London, Bodley Head 2015)

21. Mayers, David, Humanity in 1948: The Genocide Convention and the Universal Declaration of Human Rights, *Diplomacy and Statecraft*, 26, (2015)

22. McGrane, Joshua A. and White, Fiona A, Differences in Anglo and Asian Australians' Explicit and Implicit Prejudice and the Attenuation of their Implicit In-Group Bias, *Asian Journal of Social Psychology*, 10 (2007)

23. McGuinness, Margaret E, Peace v. Justice; The Universal Declaration of Human Rights and the Modern Origins of the Debate, *Diplomatic History*, 35 (5), (2011)

24. Michels, Tony, Donald Trump and the Triumph of Anti-liberalism, *Jewish Social Studies: History, Culture, Society*, 22 (3) (Spring Summer 2017)

25. Milanovic, Marko, State Responsibility for Genocide: A Follow Up, *The European Journal of International Law,* 18 (4) (2007)

26. Scholtyseck, Joachim, Fascism—National Socialism—Arab "Fascism": Terminologies, Definitions and Distinctions, *Die Welt des Islams,* 52 (2012)

27. Schmuck, Desirée and Matthes, Jörg, How Anti-immigrant Right-wing Populist Advertisements Affect Young Voters: Symbolic Threats, Economic Threats and the Moderating Role of Education, *Journal of Ethnic and Migration Studies,* 41 (10) (2015)

28. Shirer, William I, The Rise and Fall of the Third Reich, (London, Arrow 1998)

29. Slack, James, *Daily Mail,* http://www.dailymail.co.uk/news/article-3903436/Enemies-people-Furv-touch-iudges-defied-17-4m-Brexit-voters-trigger-constitutional-crisis.html, (3 November 2016)

30. Stanton, Gregory H, Genocide Watch, The Ten Stages of Genocide, http://www.genocidewatch.org/10stagesofgenocide.ppt,, (2013)

31. Ullrich, Volker, Hitler, Volume 1: Ascent (London, Bodley Head 2016)

32. Van Pelt, Robert Jan, The Case for Auschwitz: Evidence from the Irving Trial, (Indiana, Indiana University Press, 2016)

33. Wachsmann, Nicholas, KL: A History of the Nazi Concentration Camps, (London, Little Brown 2013)

34. Wheeler, Mary E and Fiske, Susan T, Controlling Racial Prejudice: Social-Cognitive Goals Affect Amygdala and Stereotype Activation, *Psychological Science,* 16 (1) (2005)

35. Whitman, James Q, Hitler's American Model, The United States and the Making of Nazi Race Law, (Princeton, Princeton University Press 2017)

36. Zillmer, Eric A, Harrower, Molly, Ritzier, Barry A, Archer, Robert P, The Quest for the Nazi Personality: A Psychological Investigation of Nazi War Criminals, (New York, Routledge 2009)

37. Zverzhanovski, Ivan, Watching War Crimes: The Srebrenica Video and the Serbian Attitudes to the 1995 Srebrenica Massacre, *Southeast European and Black Sea Studies,* 7 (3) (September 2007)

www.ingramcontent.com/pod-product-compliance
Lightning Source LLC
Chambersburg PA
CBHW070821260726
48660CB00005B/1936